Rural Sanitation: Planning and Appraisal

An OXFAM Document

compiled by Arnold Pacey
with research by Catherine Goyder

Practical
ACTION
PUBLISHING

Intermediate Technology Publications Ltd

Practical Action Publishing Ltd
27a Albert Street, Rugby, CV21 2SG, Warwickshire, UK
www.practicalactionpublishing.org

© Oxfam and Intermediate Technology Publications Ltd, 1980
Second impression

First published in 1980
Transferred to digital printing in 2008

ISBN 978 0 90303 172 1

A catalogue record for this book is available from the British Library.

Since 1974, Practical Action Publishing has published and disseminated books
and information in support of international development work throughout the
world. Practical Action Publishing
(formerly ITDG Publishing) is a trading name of Intermediate Technology
Publications Ltd
(Company Reg. No. 1159018), the wholly owned publishing company of
Intermediate Technology Development Group Ltd (working name Practical
Action). Practical Action Publishing trades only in support of its parent charity
objectives and any profits are covenanted back to Practical Action
(Charity Reg. No. 247257, Group VAT Registration No. 880 9924 76).

Contents

page

Acknowledgements 5
Preface and Summary of Contents 6
Reference Key 7

1. Introduction
Appraisal for appropriate technology 9
Two case-studies 12

2. The Appraisal of Options for Sanitation
Environmental checklists 16
Health data 20
Housing and social priorities 21
The appraisal of traditional technology 25
Appraisal and health education 28
Appraisal in perspective 31

3. Planning Technical Assistance
Material back-up for health education 32
Paying for better sanitation 36
Extension work and technical assistance 38
Technical assistance for latrine construction 40

4. Approaches to Latrine Design
Available types of latrine 46
Choosing latrines for a rural situation 50
The construction of the floor slab 53
Earthen floor slabs 57
Design of privy huts 59

5. Evaluation of Results
Monitoring long-term benefits 63
Conclusion 66

Bibliography 67

List of Illustrations

		page
Fig.1.	Cartoon drawings used for health education work in Zaire.	13
Fig.2.	Traditional housing in Serowe, Botswana.	22
Fig.3.	Low-cost housing with latrines built to similar standards in in Gaberones, Botswana (photograph).	23
Fig.4.	A traditional 'open latrine' in Bangladesh (photograph).	26
Fig.5.	Cooking in West Africa.	35
Fig.6.	Detail of ferrocement water tanks near Bulawayo, Zimbabwe (photograph).	39
Fig.7.	Ferrocement water tanks near Bulawayo, Zimbabwe (photograph).	40
Fig.8.	A simple form of pit latrine.	41
Fig.9.	A pit latrine with a vent pipe.	42
Fig.10.	Soakage pit latrine with water seal.	47
Fig.11.	The principle of the aqua-privy.	49
Fig.12.	A simple concrete floor slab.	55
Fig.13.	Concrete floor slab used in Nigeria, showing how it is made in two parts for easier handling.	56
Fig.14.	Constructing a pit latrine in Bangladesh.	58
Fig.15.	Illustration used in health education work in Zaire showing a privy hut built of concrete blocks.	60
Fig.16.	Latrine without privy hut used in Mozambique.	61

List of Tables

	page
1. The outlook of those who plan sanitation projects compared with the views of local people.	11
2. Environmental checklist part I – The village.	16
3. Environmental checklist part II – The home and family.	17
4. Improvements in hygiene and sanitation in relation to the control of specific diseases.	19
5. Materials and utensils for better hygiene.	33
6. Some criteria for the appropriateness of different types of latrine.	54

Acknowledgements

This booklet reflects the knowledge of people with far more experience than I possess; my task has been to tap their knowledge by studying field reports from their projects and by interviews and correspondence. Markedly different points of view have emerged from this exercise which I have attempted to interpret and reconcile. Thus views expressed here are my responsibility and should not be attributed to any of the following people who have helped me. First among these is Jim Howard, whose contribution has been considerable. I am also indebted to Alan J. Taylor, Alastair White, Gaby Taylor, and to several doctors in Zaire who have answered queries by letter. Some ideas expressed in this booklet were argued over during the Oxfam/Ross Institute sanitation conference held in Oxford in July 1977, and during a conference on appraisal methods at the Institute of Development Studies, Brighton, in December 1979; I am grateful to many participants at both conferences.

In addition, I have greatly benefited from the laborious researches in Oxfam project files undertaken by Catherine Goyder, and from a translation of Vietnamese material loaned by Joan K. McMichael of the organization Medical and Scientific Aid to Vietnam. I am also grateful for the extensive work carried out by the publisher's staff, who have improved the style of the text beyond recognition.

Finally, for permission to reproduce tables and illustrations I am grateful to:
UNICEF, New Delhi (for Tables 2 and 3);
Dr J. Courtejoie, Kangu-Mayumbe, Zaire (for Figs 1 and 15);
John Wiley & Sons, U.K. (for Fig.13);
IVS Package Program, Sylhet, Bangladesh (for Fig.14);
WHO, Geneva (for Fig.16).

Arnold Pacey

Funds for the printing of this booklet were made available by OXFAM and their assistance is gratefully acknowledged.

Intermediate Technology Publications Ltd.

Preface and Summary of Contents

This booklet is written for hospital staff and community development workers in Third World countries who may be planning programmes to improve sanitation or hygiene in the rural areas. It examines two important concepts which are not often discussed in the context of sanitation: the *appraisal* of a particular rural community's skills, resources and needs (Chapter 2); and the *planning* of village-level *technical assistance* to support health education (Chapter 3).

This is the third* in a series of booklets on 'socially appropriate technology', and one of its purposes is to discuss the relationship between *technology* and *social organization*. Questions about organization within a village as they affect the people's sanitation and hygiene habits have to be asked during the assessment of local needs and traditional technology and so are described principally in the chapter on appraisal and assessment (Chapter 2). Following that, the discussion of technical assistance in Chapter 3 raises questions on how the sanitation programmes themselves are organized. In this chapter, and also in Chapter 1, comment is made on the role of village health workers, technicians, and outside experts.

Although the term 'sanitation' can, strictly speaking, cover water supply as well as excreta disposal, it has been assumed here that programmes focused on sanitation will not be concerned with major improvements to village water supplies. They might, however, deal with the smaller improvements that an individual householder may make. Therefore, this booklet does include brief notes on household water supplies, mentioning backyard wells, small water filters, and in particular, rainwater storage tanks. However, these subjects are considered from the standpoint of planning, not technology. In fact, there is only one detailed technological case study in the booklet, in Chapter 4, which deals with several important aspects in the design of latrines. It should be possible to build a pit latrine of the simplest type from the information given, although for greater technical detail, one of the handbooks listed in the bibliography should be consulted.

As with the other booklets in this series, I have tried to the greatest possible extent to quote from experience gained from practical projects. Any statements based on these are indicated in the text by quoting project code numbers, for which a reference key is given on page 7. Most of the projects have been directly supported by Oxfam, but a few others are included which were discussed in detail at the Oxfam/Ross Institute conference on sanitation in 1977.

*The first and second booklets in the series were:
Hand Pump Maintenance, published 1977 and reprinted in 1980.
Gardening for Better Nutrition, published 1978.
Both were published by Intermediate Technology Publications Ltd., and are available from them at 9 King Street, London WC2E 8HN, U.K.

Reference Key

Most of the following index numbers denote Oxfam project files. In addition, though, the code FWT refers to projects quoted in the book 'Ferrocement Water Tanks' by Simon Watt. The initials SDC refer to 'Sanitation in Developing Countries', an Oxfam/Ross Institute conference report with figures following the initials to denote the page numbers in the report. Details of both publications are given in the bibliography.

BRZ 101   Brazil, House-building at Limoeiro do Norte, Ceara.
BRZ 104   Brazil, Movimento de Organisacao Comunitaria, Feira de Santana, Bahia.
BRZ 111   Brazil, Centro de Desenvolvimento, Teresina, Piaui.
BRZ 147   Brazil, Revolving loan fund, Cabrobo, Pernambuco.
DEL 2   India, Holy Family Hospital, Delhi.
FWT 1   Zimbabwe, Henson water tank project.
FWT 2   Mali, Water granaries at Sanga.
KER 17   India, Marianad Community Development Project, Puthencurichy, Trivandrum, Kerala.
RHO 10   Zimbabwe, Friends Rural Training Centre, Hlekweni, near Bulawayo; this project overlaps with FWT 1 and RHO 8 (not quoted).
SDC 94   Nigeria, Pit latrine programmes, Ishara District.
SDC 102   Zimbabwe, Rural programmes of the Blair Research Laboratory, Causeway, Salisbury.
SDC 105   St. Lucia (West Indies), Rockefeller Foundation, Castries.
SDC 113   Vietnam, Ministry of Health composting latrine programme.
SDC 167   China, Patriotic and Hygienic Campaign Committee, Shantung Province.
SDC 180   India, West Bengal village surveys.
SOM 10   Somalia, Government Basic Health Services.
TAN 73   Tanzania, Namanyere Hospital, Mbeya.
ZAI 32   Zaire, Vanga Baptist Hospital, Bandundu.
ZAI 53A   Zaire, Medical Centre, Kingoyi Mission.
ZAI 60   Zaire, Nsona Mpangu Hospital, Bas Zaire.
ZAI 67A   Zaire, Centre Medical de Kisantu (CEMEKI), Bas Zaire.
ZAI 112   Zaire, Panzi Hospital, Kwango, Bandundu.

1. Introduction

Appraisal for appropriate technology

Wherever there are problems of bad sanitation in rural areas, with all the sickness and disease that results, one may be tempted to assume that improved technology is the answer, and that new latrines will provide the necessary 'technological fix'. But technology by itself does not solve anything, and in rural areas of developing countries it is often found that latrines, when built, are not fully used, and when used, do not always banish the diseases of bad sanitation. The essential point is that good sanitation depends primarily on people, and on how they organize hygiene-related activities. Efforts to improve hygiene through health education and changes in organization are always important, therefore, regardless of what technology is used. Good sanitation depends on a large 'package' of hygiene measures, and latrines are not necessarily the part of this package most urgently required.

Even so, technology does have a part to play, and many rural communities do need help with their sanitation problems. Very basic technical assistance is most often required, and this is described in Chapter 3. Latrines may not always be a practical possibility, but if they are, then they must be carefully designed to match local patterns of organization, as discussed in Chapter 4. In some communities, though, there may be no immediate way of tackling sanitation at all because other improvements are needed first, perhaps in housing (Chapter 2) or in health services (Chapter 5).

Appraisal of options and assessment of needs

It is obviously of prime importance to recognize where a sanitation programme will be most appropriate and at what technical level. Equally, one must be able to identify situations where other kinds of improvement are needed first. It is therefore essential that a careful *assessment* be made of the problems faced by an individual community, along with an *appraisal* of all the options for improved sanitation that are open to it.

The word 'appraisal' is normally used in connection with development to mean the examination of project plans after they have been fully worked out but before funds are released to implement them. In this booklet, however, a broader concept of appraisal is used, because the options open to a rural community include techniques based on existing skills and organization as well as new techniques which the project might introduce. The appraisal of all the options available to a community must therefore include an examination of local organization, resources and skills, and must be carried out before project plans are fully drawn up. This means that some aspects of appraisal should take place at the same time as local needs are being assessed, and should involve the investigation of local craft skills that could be useful in the project, existing beliefs and customs concerning hygiene, and water-use habits. The more that is learned about these things, the more likelihood there is of finding an appropriate form of technology or technical assistance.

Application of appropriate technology

The essence of the idea of *appropriate technology* is that equipment and techniques should be appropriate to local resources as well as to local needs. Careful appraisal of local resources and the options they represent is therefore the hallmark of any project that successfully creates an appropriate technology within a local community. However, books on this approach to technology say little about appraisal methods, which seems rather an omission. If special stress is to be laid on the appropriateness of technology, then it is also important to explain how one identifies what is appropriate. Chapter 2 describes several kinds of appraisal that might be used to investigate sanitation in rural communities.

Making programmes socially acceptable

In any work of this kind, there are always likely to be two points of view. The people who plan sanitation programmes are likely to have an expert knowledge of either medicine or engineering. They therefore look at a community's needs in a relatively specialized way which may contrast sharply with the way in which local people see their problems. The risk that new technology will not be socially acceptable or appropriate arises most strongly where experts fail to recognize – and reconcile – these different points of view. If the question is asked: 'Who will decide which technology is appropriate?', the answer ought to be that the experts and local people will come to an agreed view.

One task of appraisal work, therefore, is to collect information that clarifies the goals of the experts and the local people, and seeks common ground between them. Table 1 illustrates the kind of difference in goals and attitudes which may be found, and may help, therefore, to indicate questions that need to be asked in planning a project. With regard to cultural values, for example, Table 1 notes that people may sometimes feel that there is prestige associated with owning a latrine (or other modern equipment); it also warns that the cultural attitudes of experts can create barriers to the acceptance of new techniques. Those who may be involved in such work need to be careful that their belief in the scientific principles of hygiene does not make them arrogant. One should not pretend that one always knows what is best for other people, as *all* of their problems may not *all* be apparent.

Cultural values

Many rural communities have distinctive ways of organizing sanitation and hygiene – their own 'hygiene culture' – and it is part of the task of appraisal work to understand what this involves. Local hygiene culture may sometimes be a source of difficulty for a programme, but it may also present an opportunity, in that many communities (especially Moslem and Hindu ones) set a high value on cleanliness.

Apart from cultural values, there may be many practical issues about which experts and local people have different points of view. For example, experts may not always recognize how great a cost a project may impose on the families taking

Table 1. The outlook of those who plan sanitation projects compared with the views of local people.

This is a table adapted from work by Curtis (1978). It is suggested that you modify and extend the comments in both columns of the table to suit your local situation.

	PLANNER'S VIEW	PEOPLE'S VIEW
Practical Factors		
Objectives:	Aim for very specific improvements to environment and to health.	Generalized view of better living standards and housing.
Costs:	Costs falling on project are examined.	Cost to family, including money, time, and stress examined.
Organization:	Operation and maintenance problems; health education.	Change in habits required by new techniques.
Cultural Values		
Hygiene:	Scientific concepts of health and hygiene.	Traditional views of cleanliness and disease — religion and folk medicine.
Status:	Attitudes to poverty.	Tendency to associate status with modern technology.
Taboos:	Privacy of latrines; talking openly about sanitation.	Privacy and orientation of latrines; anal cleansing methods; sex segregation.

part. 'Low-cost' latrines, judged in terms of capital investment, may in practice be very costly to local families if, for example, they take a long time to clean, are difficult to use, or involve radical changes in organization.

Reconciling objectives

The most vital issue on which the attitudes of local people and experts may diverge concerns the goals or objectives of sanitation projects. Experts will see the main goal as the prevention of disease, and will sometimes concentrate on the control of some specific disease, such as hookworm. By contrast, the local people will usually have a far more general view of the types of improvement they expect from the project. They may judge it according to what it will contribute to their overall standard of living, in terms of convenience, comfort, cost, and status. Thus, if

11

people accept the use of a latrine, it will be because they see it as a desirable addition to their home. They will never see it *solely* as a device for protecting health.

In other words, what people want may be quite different from what one may think they need. Common ground must be sought before the project can have goals which the people and the experts share. In an extreme case, where the people seem totally uninterested in any aspect of sanitation, and see development solely as a way to acquire transistor radios and bicycles, then there is no common ground and no basis for a project. More usually, though, there will be several aspects of housing and environmental conditions where the people want improvements that are of significance for better hygiene.

Two case studies

What is needed, therefore, is *flexibility* in the planning of sanitation work. It may seem that latrines are urgently needed in a particular village. But if conditions are not right for latrine construction, one may have to be flexible and adopt simpler improvements in hygiene. It is worth remembering that sanitation is a very broad concept, and that sanitation projects can properly tackle a very wide range of problems. In fact, the word 'sanitation' refers to all measures that protect health by the elimination of dirt and the infections dirt may carry.

Health education near Delhi

The need for flexibility can be illustrated by comparing two rural sanitation programmes. In the first example, community education in hygiene was carried out by teams from an Indian hospital in villages near Delhi (DEL 2).* The hospital has experimented with many forms of educational media for conveying advice about hygiene in a vivid and persuasive way — notably using drama and mime shows at village gatherings. As the local people are too poor to build latrines for themselves, the advice offered is of a simpler kind, about wearing shoes as a precaution against hookworm, and washing hands after defecation. This is a good example of a realistic and flexible approach. One limitation, however, seems to be the time available for visits to individual homes and discussions of individual problems. This can be a vital part of health education, but tends to be left out if the health team only has a brief time to spend in the villages.

Projects in Zaire

A different approach is adopted in a series of projects undertaken in Zaire. It is usual in Zaire to recruit one or two people from each village to take part in health education activities as 'community workers' or 'village health workers'. Since these people are always on-the-spot, the problem of relying on visits from health teams is avoided. At the start of a village programme, these health workers attend a centre for about six weeks of training in hygiene and sanitation techniques (ZAI 67A).

This index number for the project is explained in the reference key at the beginning of the booklet.

12

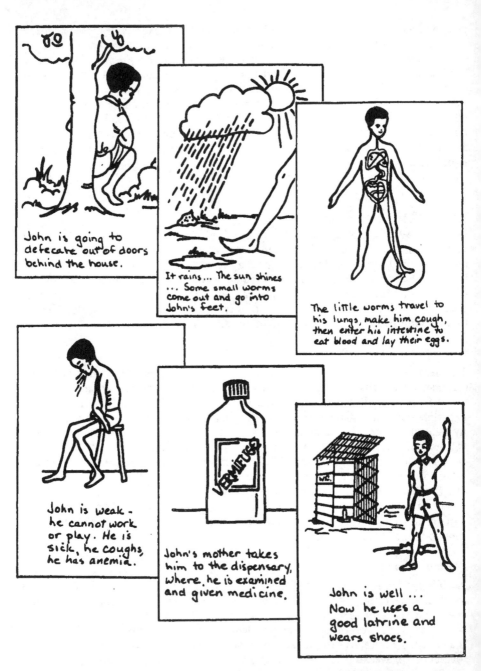

Fig.1. Cartoon drawings used for health education work in Zaire; the captions have been translated. Three measures against hookworm are emphasized — drugs, latrines, and wearing shoes. (From material developed by J. Courtejoie, C. Nzungu, and I. Rotsart de Hertaing, Health Education Centre, Kangu-Mayumbe.)

When they return to their village they carry out a variety of duties: they are invaluable as back-ups to visiting nurses giving talks on hygiene; they call on people in their homes for individual discussions, and report back to the project centre on the extent of local interest. Very often, they work with a village health committee which provides another forum for the exchange of views on local sanitation needs.

The starting point for the work in Zaire was the Vanga Hospital in Bandundu (ZAI 32). This long-established missionary hospital began public work in 1967, and by 1974 its sanitation programmes extended to 108 villages in the surrounding area. In each village, the aim has been to ensure that at least 90 per cent of all households acquire a pit latrine. Once this has been achieved, the 'entire population of the village is given a mass worm cure'. In other words, everybody is dosed with drugs which tend to kill any intenstinal worms in their bodies. The wearing of shoes as a precaution against hookworm is also encouraged, as can be seen from the visual aids used locally in health education (Fig.1).

Vanga Hospital regularly runs courses for nurses and nursing auxiliaries from other parts of Zaire, many of whom have started similar health education and sanitation programmes in their own localities. In studying reports from some half-dozen of these projects, one is struck by the success of those which involve village health workers, and the much slower progress of those which rely solely on periodic visits to villages by a health education team from the local hospital. It is also interesting that each separate project has kept to the original formula, with the emphasis on building latrines. Only one has emphasized water supplies as well (ZAI 53A), and nowhere is the washing of hands stressed to the extent noted in the Delhi case-study.

Emphasis on health problems

In the Zaire programmes, as also in the Delhi work, appraisal seems to have concentrated on health problems (mainly to do with hookworm), and on what people could afford. In neither area was the broader context of sanitation fully examined, such as its relationship to housing. The Zaire projects probably gained in sensitivity to local conditions through the work of the village health workers and local committees: even so, the responses of Zaire project teams seem to have been rather inflexible. A standard package was offered to most villages consisting of latrines and worm cures, and communities which this did not suit were not catered for. This minority of villages was described by one of the project organizers as having problems which were 'in need of further study'. He then outlined the kind of appraisal that would be undertaken to discover why some communities were unreceptive, explaining that 'villages which have participated in this programme are being compared with villages which have not . . .' (ZAI 32). This, then, is a situation where a new and deeper assessment of local needs is being made only after some people have rejected an apparently suitable sanitation technology.

Vanga Hospital and rural sanitation

The achievements of the Vanga Hospital with regard to rural sanitation have been quite exceptional. If their approaches to villages are sometimes rejected, how much more do those of us with less experience need to make thorough appraisals at the start of our work? Several questionnaires and survey methods for use in appraisal

14

are discussed in the next chapter. It is not suggested that all these approaches should be used in every situation. That would be too time-consuming. The methods chosen must depend on local circumstances, and particularly on whether village-level health workers are available to assist in surveys. Appraisals need to be fairly rapid if they are to lead to practical results, but they also need to be thorough enough to challenge the habitual assumptions of experts and prevent too much being taken for granted.

2. The Appraisal of Options for Sanitation

Environmental checklists

Planning for rural sanitation depends on information gained on various facets of the local situation, of which three of the most important are health, housing, and existing sanitary conditions. The collection of some environmental data requires specialized knowledge, but there is a good deal of important information about sanitary conditions which can be collected by village health workers.

UNICEF checklists in India

In India, UNICEF has experimented with two checklists which can help local health workers to pinpoint two or three important features of any village or individual household where sanitary improvement is especially desirable (Tables 2 and 3).

The checklists may draw attention to a variety of problems and solutions:

— to excreta disposal, food hygiene, garbage, or water supply as potential areas of

---

Table 2. Environmental Checklist Part I: The village.

(If the answer to any question is NO, this indicates a possible health hazard, probably requiring some action.)

---

1. Do people defecate so that their excreta is kept away from places where other people may walk, and where flies cannot reach them (e.g. by using a latrine or by burying the excreta)?
2. If children leave faeces near their homes, are they immediately removed?
3. Do people defecate far away from the source of drinking water?
4. Is the drinking water source *different* from the place where people and animals bathe, and women wash clothes?
5. Does the village have a protected water source, such as a protected spring, a well with a hand-pump, or a piped water supply?
6. Do people *use* water from the protected source?
7. If there is a protected water source, is it conveniently placed for everybody? If there are wells, are there enough of them? If there is a piped supply, are there enough taps?
8. Is the area around the wells or the public taps dry?
9. Do people try to ensure that stagnant water is drained away, so that the rain does not leave big puddles in the village?
10. Are there any compost pits or rubbish bins in the village?

Table 3. Environmental Checklist Part II: The home and family.

(If the answer to any question is NO, this indicates a possible health hazard, probably requiring some action.)

1. If the household has a latrine, is it clean, and is there a cover or other means of keeping flies out?
2. Is the house clean and free from flies?
3. Does the family have clean drinking water?
4. Are there containers for storing water, and are they covered and clean?
5. Is there a bowl and soap for washing hands?
6. Do people regularly wash hands after defecation and before eating?
7. Are the preferred materials for anal cleaning (e.g. paper) always available? Or if water is used, is it available near the latrine or defecation site?
8. Is there provision for young children to defecate hygienically in or near the house (e.g. a pot)?
9. If the household has cattle or other animals, is the cow-shed clean?
10. Is there a compost pit or bin where animal droppings can be safely placed, and where children's faeces can be put?
11. Does the housewife throw rubbish into a compost pit or bin?
12. Is it possible to prepare food in clean surroundings, and if there is a kitchen, is it convenient for the housewife?

---

trouble;
— to problems caused by children defecating in or near the home;
— to the need for an organized compost heap or rubbish pit where such faeces may be promptly disposed of, along with animal droppings and rubbish;
— to the potential for the improvement of kitchens so that greater cleanliness is achieved.

Range of solutions

The questions in Tables 2 and 3 are closely based on the UNICEF checklists, though with modifications to make them more generally applicable to rural areas in countries other than India. The original UNICEF version is part of a draft booklet which suggests a range of responses to the problems revealed by the checklist. For example, people may defecate in the open near a water source because they use water for cleaning themselves afterwards. But this will pollute the water and make it unsafe for drinking. It may be possible to persuade people of the dangers of this habit. They may then move their defecation ground away from the water, or downstream from the place where they collect water. Or it may be possible to persuade them to

17

start building latrines, or to dig a trench latrine for use by everybody. Any of these measures would prevent the drinking water from being polluted, and rather than opting immediately for a standardized solution, one should first consider the whole range of possibilities.

Other considerations

Obviously, though, not all of these possibilities are equally desirable. Where there is an open defecation ground, however far it may be from houses and from water, infection can be transferred to the people's homes by flies or rats or wind-blown dust. However, if well-constructed latrines are really beyond the people's means, finding a better place for the defecation ground and encouraging people to bury excreta are two measures which can protect health significantly.

The two checklists illustrated may also show that excreta disposal is not necessarily the most urgent matter needing attention. Washing habits, laundry, or hygiene in child care are also important. Thus, the range of possible improvements can be considerable, and the choice of the best combination of changes must depend on what people can afford, what is most feasible for them in terms of time and skill, and the relative urgency of the problem concerned.

Beyond the checklists

Apart from the details of village environments which can be surveyed by local health workers using checklists, there are one or two larger issues which the planners of projects should consider. One of these is population density. It has already been seen that in a rural area where population density is assumed to be low, there may be several ways of preventing excreta from polluting a water source or the home environment. Some of the options do not involve latrines but simply require a more careful choice of site for defecation in the open, and preferably also the burying of excreta. In more crowded conditions, however, this approach offers no real protection at all for the health of the people. In most towns and large villages, it is impossible to isolate excreta adequately from the environment of the people's lives except by using latrines.

In places where people are being resettled in larger villages than they are accustomed to, they tend to continue the defecation habits which they practised around their former homes. In such circumstances, habits that were once satisfactory may prove to be dangerous. In Tanzania, where many people have been resettled in 'ujamaa villages', public health workers reported an increased incidence of diseases associated with bad sanitation during the early stages of resettlement (TAN 73).

School latrines

In many communities, it may be appropriate to install latrines in schools, even if individual household privies cannot immediately be built. Not only is there likely to be a bigger health risk around schools, but it may be judged educationally useful to introduce children to the idea of using a privy. It may also be easier to ensure that cleaning of latrines is properly carried out at schools than elsewhere. Since children learn through example, it is especially important that school latrines should be kept

18

thoroughly clean. One project which has stressed the importance of sanitation at village schools works on the basis that there should be one latrine for every forty children (ZAI 60).

Health data

Hospital staff and other people employed by health services in rural areas are often struck by the prevalence of diseases that appear to be associated with deficient hygiene or sanitation. For this reason, it is often nurses or doctors who initiate rural sanitation programmes, and their chief aim is usually to match the type of sanitation available to the health problems which seem most urgent in the area concerned. Sometimes, they will carry out a systematic survey of disease incidence before planning their sanitation work in detail. Then a similar survey can be made later to check whether the improvement in sanitation has, in fact, benefited health. But even where medical staff do not have the resources to undertake such systematic researches, their knowledge of local patterns of disease will give them an idea of the type of sanitary improvement which may be most beneficial.

Classifying diseases

Members of the Ross Institute in London have developed an approach to matching sanitation measures and patterns of disease with much greater clarity than existed previously. They have classified the diseases associated with deficient hygiene, water supply, and waste disposal according to the most relevant steps that can be taken to prevent them. There is not enough space here to go into the technicalities of the Ross Institute classification — further detail can be found in the relevant works by Bradley, Feachem, and Hawkins listed in the bibliography.

Table 4 lists many of the diseases discussed by these authors, and indicates the improvements in hygiene and sanitation that are likely to have the biggest impact on the prevalence of each.

Inevitably, this single, compact table greatly simplifies the thinking on which it is based. For example, the effect of improving water supply is often complex. The diarrhoeal diseases, dysentery and gastro-enteritis are each transmitted by several different routes. So it cannot be said with certainty which improvements in water supply will affect them most. However, much experience seems to show that the use of greatly increased volumes of water for washing has most benefit, even where the water is not very pure.

By contrast, the protection of water against pollution, or its thorough disinfection, is absolutely crucial where there is a high risk of cholera or typhoid. Protection of water sources against contamination by people collecting water is also a necessary precaution against guinea worm — though where water from an unprotected source must be used, filtration of the water will be effective. Indeed, guinea worm is the only infection for which filtration is a fully effective precaution.

It is widely recognized that parasitic worm infections may be prevented, in most instances, by efficient excreta disposal, but Table 4 adds some details and qualifications to this generalization. For example, it stresses the importance of

19

Table 4. Improvements in hygiene and sanitation in relation to the control of specific diseases.

xx denotes the improvements likely to be most effective;
x   denotes other relevant improvements.

DISEASE	MEASURES LIKELY TO BE EFFECTIVE			
	Improved excreta disposal	Improved water supply	More thorough washing	Better food hygiene
Waterborne and washing-related diseases				
Typhoid) Cholera)	x[1]	xx[2]	x[4]	x
Amoebic dysentery) Bacillary dysentery) Diarrhoeal diseases) Gastro-enteritis) Infectious hepatitis)	x[1]	xx	xx[4]	xx
Washing-related infections of skin and eyes				
Skin sepsis & ulcers) Conjunctivitis) Trachoma) Scabies)	—	xx[3]	xx	—
Parasitic worm infections				
Bilharzia (Schistosomiasis)	xx	x	—	—
Guinea worm	—	xx[2]	—	—
Hookworm (*Necator*)[6]	xx[1]	—	—	—
Hookworm (*Ancylostoma*)[6]	xx[1]	x	x[4]	x
Roundworm (*Ascaris*)	xx[1]	x	xx[4]	x
Tapeworm (*Taenia spp.*)	xx	—	—	xx[5]

Notes:
1. Ensure scrupulous cleanliness of latrines;
2. The priority is to protect the water source from pollution or to purify the water;
3. The priority is to supply greater volumes of water;
4. Washing of hands after defecation and before meals is especially relevant;
5. Cook meat thoroughly to destroy infection;
6. The wearing of shoes is an effective precaution against both kinds of hookworm.

keeping latrines clean. This should be taken as a warning against some 'low-cost' privies which are incapable of being cleaned adequately, often because of rough or porous floors. Speaking of hookworm, Hawkins and Feachem* comment that 'unless they are very clean, the latrines themselves may easily become efficient foci for transmission'. And regarding roundworm, 'the higher incidence . . . among urban latrine users as compared with rural non-users has been attributed to dirty latrines'.

In many rural communities, therefore, existing forms of excreta disposal may be preferable to latrines until such time that a very high standard of construction and cleanliness is feasible. Until then it may be best to foster other means of improving general hygiene.

Sanitary precautions

With several diseases, the washing of hands after defecation is a particularly relevant precaution, but another consideration should be the way in which laundry is done, especially where soiled baby clothing has to be dealt with. Better laundry may be relevant, too, with regard to the skin and eye diseases mentioned in the table, because unwashed towels and clothing shared between members of a family may transmit the infections.

What Table 4 cannot show is the full range of sanitary precautions that may be taken. For example, one preventive measure against bilharzia (schistosomiasis) is to eliminate the water snails which are the intermediate host for the parasite causing this illness. This, however, will often be beyond the scope of small projects. More significantly, the table does not mention refuse disposal, the control of rats, drainage, or composting. In places where excreta is traditionally used for fertilizer, composting can be introduced as a means of reducing the health risks to farmers or to people eating the produce. Refuse disposal and drainage are important in reducing the breeding sites available to flies and mosquitoes, and may be relevant measures against many diarrhoeal diseases where flies are prevalent, or against malaria and filariasis where mosquitoes abound.

Despite its limitations, however, Table 4 should help in the choice of sanitation improvements which may be most beneficial in any particular locality. It should also emphasize that no single improvement is likely to be effective by itself. One needs generally to consider how people might combine a material improvement with better washing habits, food hygiene and better personal hygiene. Where the worm infections are concerned, it may also be relevant to provide medical treatment that will help rid people of these parasites.

Housing and social priorities

The surveys of environmental conditions and disease incidence which have so far been discussed should help to clarify the goals of sanitation projects. This, however,

For all references to work by named authors, details of the book or article concerned can be found in the bibliography at the end of this booklet.

will be somewhat one-sided because, as seen in Chapter 1, local people do not always look at a programme's goals and objectives in the same way as those who plan the programme. People may be less interested in theoretical benefits to health than in the visible betterment of their general living conditions, a distinction emphasized by Table 1.

Recognizing priorities

It needs to be recognized, then, that the people will have their own social priorities. For example, in one region of Brazil, householders have been encouraged to build pit latrines for themselves after saving the money to buy materials. However, it has been found that the completed privies are not always used for defecation. Instead, they become places where the family valuables are stored — bicycles, transistor radios, pots and pans. This is because the latrine huts are much better constructed than the houses, and, very often, the privy is the only room with a door that can be locked. So the people see the goal of the project as being connected with home improvements, and not with health.

In such circumstances, although latrines may be urgently needed to prevent disease, there is no point in building them — at least, not until the houses can also be rebuilt. As disillusioned community workers in Brazil have commented, it does not make sense to see well-built, subsidized privy huts alongside cardboard and mud shanties with leaking roofs. In any case, there may be more urgent health priorities, too. One health worker said, 'What's the use of conning people into building privies when they don't even eat enough to use them very often?' (BRZ 104).

Latrines in Botswana

In the small towns and large villages of Botswana, conditions have been much more

Fig.2. Traditional housing in Serowe, Botswana. A sketch showing the buildings which together formed the home of one family in 1972. The pit latrine (on the right) and the hut with the window (on the left) had just been completed. The low structure in the left foreground is a cooking shelter.

Fig.3. Low-cost housing with latrines built to similar standards in Gaberones, Botswana. Note the ample ventilation space below the roofs of the privy huts. (Photo: Arnold Pacey.)

favourable for the introduction and use of latrines. Many pit latrines have been constructed by householders in the process of improving their homes. There are examples of this in the small, semi-rural town of Serowe, where most houses are of traditional construction with neat mud-brick walls and thatched roofs. Such houses are being modernized in many detailed ways: glass windows and lockable doors are being fitted, and more furniture obtained. Pit latrines are often added as part of the same scheme. Fig.2 shows one family's compound as it stood in 1972. The living accommodation consisted of two thatched huts, which were well-furnished with beds, a table, and chairs. One of the huts had just been rebuilt with a glass window, and at the same time a pit latrine had been constructed.

In the larger settlements, where municipal low-cost housing has been built, the accommodation is often less generous than where traditional housing is still the norm. Nevertheless, the opportunity has been taken to provide privies of the same standard of construction as the dwellings (see Fig.3).

Experience in many countries confirms that once improvements in housing begin to take place, the people's interest in latrines as another aspect of the improvement can be more easily aroused. But where latrines are introduced before it has been possible to improve housing, they are less acceptable, or are not used for the purpose intended.

The question of cost

Closely related to this social observation is the economic question of whether people can afford household privies. It has been suggested that the cost of a privy should not exceed 10 per cent of the total cost of building the family home.

Judged by this criterion, it would seem that few people in rural areas of developing countries can afford a sufficiently well-constructed latrine for the effective protection of their health. Excellent latrines have been tried out in Tanzania which cost US$300 each (in 1978); but this is a very large figure in relation to the cost of local houses, and out-of-reach for most rural families.

The family in Botswana whose home is illustrated in Fig.2 kept careful accounts of how much they had spent on building their new hut with the glass window; the total came to the equivalent of US$105 (1972 exchange rate). Since the family lived in two such buildings, their total investment in housing can be estimated to be about $200. This, of course, ignores the considerable investment of the family's own labour in erecting the structure. The cost of their pit latrine, again excluding labour, was probably $20-30, which is just over the recommended 10 per cent of housing costs.

It is now clear why appraisal surveys should pay particular attention to a community's houses. They provide a useful indication of the kind of sanitation programme which is likely to be most useful to the people, especially with regard to costs, materials available for construction, and attitudes to the improvement of the home environment. If houses are being actively improved, this may indicate that people also have the resources and interest to build latrines.

This relationship between improving housing and the people's interest in sanitation underlines the point made previously about the objectives of sanitation programmes: because many people look on sanitation as part of their overall living conditions, they may acquire latrines for much the same reasons as they do glass windows or furniture. Although they may often be aware of the health benefits latrines are supposed to confer, these may be regarded as rather intangible compared with matters of convenience or status.

Importance of communication with individuals

Obviously one should not just rely on looking at houses and improvements to houses when assessing the likely attitude of the people to sanitation. Every opportunity should be taken to talk with people about home improvements or health problems. Formal occasions for discussion may be provided by village meetings or health education sessions, as will be mentioned again at the end of this chapter. However, people probably reveal more about their ultimate aspirations during informal conversation, and a good deal may be learnt by staying in the village for a while and spending some leisure time with the community — it would be even better if visits were made to individual homes.

Compromising

Whatever aspirations for the improvement of living standards people may have, it needs to be recognized that these are valid social priorities. A sanitation programme which conflicts with such priorities is likely to fail — but a programme which complements what people already want to do about improving their homes may hope for wide social acceptance and support. This may mean that plans for latrines have to take second place to other home improvements. However, the modernization of houses may present opportunities for better food hygiene or general cleanliness which can be quite properly supported by sanitation workers.

The appraisal of traditional technology

One aim of an appraisal survey should be to look for local skills which might help in providing better sanitation. For example, there may be a potter in the area able to make chamber pots, pans for simple water-seal latrines, bowls for washing, tiles, or household filters for drinking water. Techniques used in building houses may suggest ways in which privies can be built or water obtained. In many parts of Africa, very remarkable techniques exist for using mud or clay in building. Soil is mixed with other materials (such as cassava flour) to make a 'cement' which sets very hard. This has been successfully used in building latrines, as will be explained in Chapter 4.

Building techniques used in Mali

Techniques based on this type of material are widely used among the Dogon people of Mali (West Africa), whose houses have flat roofs with an outlet for rainwater on one side. An opportunity for collecting this water for domestic use was suggested by large, mud-walled grain bins which stand near the houses. Methods were developed for lining these bins with waterproof ferrocement, turning them into tanks or 'water granaries' (FWT 2). Large volumes of rainwater can now be collected, and tanks made partly of mud walling are much cheaper than those made entirely of ferrocement.

This merging of a traditional craft method with imported technology depended very much on the responsiveness of experts from outside the village to local craft skills. The philosophy of the project which achieved this was not 'modernization', but rather the 'organic development of a traditional society' (see Guggenheim and Fanale 1976). Villagers were consulted at every stage, and imported western techniques were radically transformed when combined with local methods.

Water supply in Nigeria

Other interesting water supply methods are to be found in parts of Nigeria which have more rain than Mali, and where there is a long tradition of rainwater harvesting from sloping roofs thatched with palm leaves. A typical house might have a small central courtyard, with the roofs arranged to direct water into a tank occupying most of this space. Usually, there is an overflow drain leading through the foundations of the building, and in older Yoruba houses this is sometimes connected to an underground tank.

Other water supply techniques

In many other countries, simple methods are in use for collecting rainwater from roofs, and these have potential for development. In Ghana, for instance, guttering is sometimes made from split bamboos.

Where people have to carry all their water from a distant source in pots and buckets, they may never collect enough for adequate hygiene in their homes, so

Fig.4. A traditional 'open latrine' in Bangladesh. It offers some privacy to its users, but is a considerable danger to their health. It relies on the slope of the ground to drain excreta into the weed-choked pond behind. (Photo: Nick Fogden, Oxfam.)

any method that supplements this supply is welcome. In some places, watertight leather bags are made to be slung over the backs of oxen or donkeys, greatly increasing the amount of water that can be carried. There may be some potential for extending this technique to other places where leather is available, or large oil-drums may be used to carry water on animal-drawn vehicles.

In some places where the only available water is dirty, there are traditional techniques for improving its quality. In parts of South America, crushed bark from certain trees is added to water. Elsewhere, various seeds are used, or curd from sour milk, and in parts of India leaves from the neem tree. Such substances usually only affect the taste of the water, although some could make the water marginally safer to use and they need not be discouraged.

Traditional latrines in rural areas

Although many rural communities have been content with very basic methods of excreta disposal, in some regions there are long traditions of latrine construction. In West Africa, for instance, latrines are a traditional feature of the larger and older houses in some towns, and communal latrines are found in some villages. In Bangladesh there are 'open latrines' which give a little privacy for defecation but are very unhygienic (Fig.4).

Elsewhere in Asia, latrines have been used for a long time as a means of collecting excreta for use as fertilizer. Because they are designed to produce fertilizer rather than promote hygiene, these latrines may be very unsatisfactory from a health point of view. Still, where they do exist, one can at least expect that the habit of regular latrine use is well established. This is a positive feature which may make it easier for people to adjust to a new type of latrine. The structure and materials for existing latrines may also be worth examining with a view to their use with more modern equipment.

Other sanitary techniques

Apart from traditional latrines, there may be other local sanitary techniques which should be noted. In Western countries, sanitary equipment includes many ancillary items: chamber pots and nappies for children, sanitary towels for women, toilet paper and bidets for cleaning oneself, basins for washing hands, and special brushes and chemicals for cleaning latrines. In a developing rural area, few of these will be available, but the functions that many of them fulfil must still be met. The expatriate sanitation engineer frequently has little information about these matters, yet some of them may be crucial. Where solid materials such as corn-cobs are used for anal cleaning, they may easily block latrines of certain kinds. Even more important, where there are no nappies or potties for use by children, the improvement in hygiene made by any kind of sanitation system may be marginal, as children's faeces are often highly infective, and may be deposited almost randomly wherever they are at play.

One particular problem of studying traditional techniques is that some important aspects may be easily overlooked. This is particularly true where people organize excreta disposal in such a way that they compensate for a comparative lack of sanitation equipment by good discipline. One may notice the lack of equipment and conclude that the community has no real sanitation technology, but it may be wiser to recognize the significance of local organization in coping with sanitary problems and to realise that the people have good 'software' but very little 'hardware'.

Sanitation equipment in China

The most impressive examples of this are probably to be found in China, where sanitation equipment in rural areas is still very crude, often consisting of very shallow pit latrines, bucket latrines, or receptacles similar to chamber pots. These devices are emptied manually into buckets, often using scoops or ladles. All this would seem to involve a considerable health hazard due to spillage. Yet since the 1950s, China has made great strides in reducing the incidence of excreta-related diseases such as bilharzia, hookworm, and gastro-enteritis. This has been achieved by employing large numbers of people in sanitation teams to empty and clean latrines and to supervise the hygienic composting of wastes. In other words, better hygiene has been achieved by strengthening the organization and discipline of sanitation, even where the resources to replace relatively primitive hardware were lacking (SDC 167).

Sanitation in Bengal

A more typical example of sanitation 'software' comes from a group of villages in West Bengal (India) where latrines are almost non-existent. Most people instead use specific areas of land which are recognized defecation grounds, and do so in a highly orderly manner (SDC 180). One of the principal excreta-related diseases in the area is hookworm, and though the spread of this is not totally prevented by the way in which the defecation grounds are used, the disease is controlled to a very significant degree. It seems unlikely that simple, low-cost latrines could offer much advantage over existing arrangements; so until full sanitation can be afforded, the most promising form of development is to accept the way defecation is currently organized, and to make detailed improvements within that context. One such improvement suggested by a local expert was to plough the defecation grounds periodically, leaving them with a furrowed surface (SDC 180).

Appraisal and health education

The appraisal of traditional technology presents no problem as long as one is concerned with physical objects: tools, pottery, houses, granaries. Questions about how such items are made or used can easily be added to check-lists such as those in Tables 2 and 3 (pages 16 and 17). But software − the organizational aspect of technology − is more difficult to assess. People may not be very keen to discuss some matters, and many aspects of behaviour in hygiene are carried out in private. There are, of course, some visible aspects of hygiene that one can look out for, perhaps prompted by the check-lists. For example, questions 2 and 6 in Table 2 raise some issues of behaviour and organization.

One other way of learning which customs prevail is to live in the village oneself for a few days. When I stayed in a rural community in Swaziland, it seemed advisable to ask a local person where to defecate. Since the question was prompted by personal need rather than curiosity, I received a frank and practical answer. All that the people there expected was a degree of privacy, behind bushes and away from paths, and there was no organized system.

Two-way exchange of ideas

Very often, though, the best way of finding out in detail about matters of organization will be through the educational activities which are an essential part of most sanitation programmes. Those responsible for health education usually hold village meetings, attend village committees, arrange talks for mothers attending clinics, hold discussions with village elders, and recruit local people to train as village health workers. All these channels for conveying information *to* the community can also be used as sources of information, and as means of learning *from* the community. Indeed, people will often be more receptive to advice about hygiene if they find that those who offer the advice are willing to listen as well as to instruct. A two-way exchange of ideas is always more stimulating than just listening to a lecture.

Thus, the way to start a discussion about hygiene might be by inviting people to explain their ideas and beliefs about cleanliness and health. Beginning with the local person's knowledge, such a discussion might well lead to an increased understanding

28

on both sides about the reasons for existing customs and how they might be changed. This kind of dialogue ought probably to cover washing habits, all aspects of water use, defecation habits, and food hygiene. The aim should be to bring together the expert's knowledge of how diseases spread and the local person's knowledge of the village environment and village customs. One can then gradually build up a body of knowledge about health in the local community which will be far more specific and useful than an abstract knowledge of the scientific principles of health.

Teaching by example

People's interest in better sanitation should increase with their knowledge, but they will be further influenced if leading members of the village are seen to adopt the new practices. It is important, therefore, to find out whether the local school-master, priest, herbalist, or headman could set this kind of example. It would also be useful if there is a village midwife who has a particular influence with local women.

As part of an appraisal, therefore, it is important to identify the leaders of opinion in the community. It is also important to note the community's traditions and customs, because people may find new hygiene practices easier to adopt if they can be seen as a simple extension of an existing custom. In many communities, there will be occasions such as visiting the temple or sitting down to a meal which are preceded by thorough washing. If such customs exist, it may be possible to strengthen them. Sometimes, the habit of washing after defecation can be encouraged as an extension of these traditional washing habits.

Working with women

In seeking information, and in all health education work, there is a strong case for trying to work with women rather than with men, since it is the women who are most involved in the practice of hygiene. They are the ones who carry water, prepare food, do the laundry, and wash the children. The problem of how and where children defecate will usually be among the most difficult matters to tackle as well as among the most important for health. Women are more likely to be able to find solutions for this than men. For these reasons, it is crucially important that women are well-represented on any village committee or working group, and it may be important also to recruit a woman as the village health worker. Similarly, the poorer sections of the community should be adequately represented; if the committee is drawn only from the upper stratum, it is less likely to understand the behaviour of the poorer people.

Village health committees

A village health committee is likely to provide good opportunities for the pooling of expert and local knowledge. It is here, then, that the principles of sanitation might first be explained, with whatever visual aids and demonstrations that can be provided. Such demonstrations should lead straight into discussion of the local relevance of the principles mentioned, raising questions which will elicit information needed by the project team, as well as helping the people to appreciate what is involved. Discussions could attempt to cover some of the following points:

a. is there any contradiction between the scientific ideas presented and the beliefs that people already have?
b. what habits of hygiene are currently followed? Which have positive value and can be used to foster better sanitation? Which may be harming health?
c. are people *consistent* in following recognized customs?
d. what health hazards arise from local environmental conditions?
e. what kinds of betterment in living conditions do people most want? What are their attitudes to 'modernization' and to 'tradition'?

Tackling traditional beliefs

Some of these subjects will need to be discussed with tact, which is one reason for raising them first in a small group or committee. When trying to find out about personal hygiene habits, it is obviously best not to ask a person 'what do you do?', but 'what is generally done?'. And in discussing matters of religion and traditional belief, it is wise not to press people too far. If it is apparent that there is some conflict between scientific views and traditional beliefs, it may be useful to have a private talk with the local religious leader or practitioner of folk medicine, who may be able to re-interpret the traditional view. The health educator should not regard it as his or her task to 'break down' traditional beliefs, but to discover where they have positive value for sanitation and build on that.

Habits connected with technology

The appraisal of local beliefs, customs and social structures is a complicated matter. Of greatest interest, perhaps, are the habits and forms of organization which are directly connected with the use of technology. This 'software' element includes the way in which work is organized, especially its allocation between the sexes, which often leaves women with the greatest responsibility in matters of hygiene. One needs to ask 'would better sanitation add to the women's burden, e.g. in the work of cleaning latrines?' 'What provisions are being made for the special and urgent needs of children, and how will this affect their mothers?' The replacement of traditional techniques by better sanitation may demand changes in other habits too, perhaps affecting the times when people defecate and wash. Therefore, it is important to understand the extent of the changes that people are asked to make.

Studying social details

In many small sanitation projects, a full study of all these social details is not possible. Very often, this aspect of the work will be left to a nurse or community worker who has specialized in health education. Such a person often has considerable experience, and may intuitively achieve good insight into the local point of view. He or she will then often do a good job with very limited resources.

In larger projects, however, it will usually be desirable for somebody with training in anthropology or social work to give a lead to this part of the programme. With considerable humility, two engineers have commented that: 'Excreta disposal in rural areas is far more complex socially than it is technically, and it is not appropriate to assign total responsibility for rural sanitation programmes to engineers'

(Feachem and Cairncross 1978). They go on to say that teamwork is required to link the efforts of engineers, community development workers and health personnel, possibly under the leadership of the community workers, because the latter have the 'closest contact with the people'.

Appraisal in perspective

In this chapter and the previous one, five subjects have been suggested for appraisal or assessment in connection with rural sanitation programmes:

— environmental conditions;
— the incidence of disease;
— housing;
— traditional technology; and
— the social organization of hygiene.

Possible ways of studying these subjects have been discussed at some length, because appraisal is rarely dealt with adequately in technical literature. However, it would be wrong to think that elaborate researches are needed on all the subjects in every programme. The purpose of appraisal is *not* to produce exhaustive information, but to check the basic objectives of the programme, to challenge unwarranted assumptions, and above all to help outsiders to see the local person's point of view.

The purpose of appraisal, then, is practical — it is to find out the kinds of rural development which are likely to be relevant, acceptable and feasible. In the context of this booklet, therefore, appraisal is a means of identifying the most appropriate options for improving rural sanitation. The only aspect of the work which cannot be rushed is the collection of data about social aspects of sanitation. This task can sometimes be started in advance of other parts of the programme, or can be built into ongoing health education work. Much can be gained by employing village-level health workers to collect information, but time has to be allowed for their training (up to six weeks).

Specialized knowledge of sanitation may help us to see what is ideally necessary for a particular community, but it is also necessary to find out the kind of programme which will best gain the people's support. Therefore, it is necessary to balance views of the ideal against local views on general living standards, perhaps with the help of Table 1 (p.11). To gain the fullest possible insight into the people's attitudes, knowledge, and capabilities, one should listen to their opinions, look at their housing, and study their craft skills.

3. Planning Technical Assistance

Material back-up for health education

Sanitation programmes are likely to include four distinct kinds of work: appraisal, health education, technical assistance, and design of equipment. Of these, the design or choice of equipment — a topic discussed in the next chapter — is the most specialized. Since not every project needs to introduce equipment new to a community, the need for this activity does not always arise. That leaves three activities which are typical of most sanitation programmes, and among these, health education is usually the most prominent and important. Good sanitation depends most of all on people, and on their organization and habits. If people are to be reached and their habits modified, health education is essential.

Health education that is based on a dialogue with the people, and not just on instructing them, provides an important channel for learning about the local situation, and for making an appraisal of project opportunities. Indeed, experience gained from health education work has often been the starting point for rural sanitation projects.

It may come as a surprise, then, that there is no chapter on educational methods in this booklet. One reason is that a good deal has already been said about health education in the discussion on appraisal methods in the last chapter, and also in Chapter 1 (see especially Fig.1 on p.13). In addition, this chapter on technical assistance in rural areas, also deals indirectly with health education. The very term 'technical assistance' denotes practical help that is designed to back up the health educator's efforts. For example, health talks might be given at village meetings advising people about the importance of washing their hands with soap after defecating, but this advice will be wasted if they lack soap, or bowls for washing, or containers for carrying water. If health education is to be taken seriously, deficiencies of this sort that make hygiene impossible must be tackled in a practical way. And that is technical assistance in its simplest form.

There are several approaches to excreta disposal which may be adopted in health education work, calling for different levels of technical assistance. If villagers are advised to build latrines for themselves, they may need a considerable amount of practical help, but if they are encouraged to adopt simpler measures, they may instead need chamber pots (potties) for children or hoes and shovels for burying wastes.

Even considering just the simpler measures which health educators may encourage, excluding latrine construction and water supplies, there is still a surprising variety of materials and utensils which people may need for the practice of better hygiene. Table 5 is not a complete list, but indicates a wide range of possible items.

As part of the initial assessment of local resources, it might be useful to check how many of these things people already possess. At the same time, items which might easily be supplied locally should be noted. Obviously, though, most projects will

Table 5. Materials and utensils for better hygiene.

Materials or utensils required	Comments on use
1. Defecation and waste disposal	
Digging hoe or spade, also shovel	For burying faeces, making compost pits, or making simple latrines (e.g. Fig.16)
Chamber pots	Usually for children
Nappies or equivalent	For children
Toilet paper or equivalent	Not in areas where water is used for anal cleaning
2. Washing hands after defecation or before meals	
Soap	
Bowls	
Towelling	
3. Hookworm precautions	
Shoes or other footwear	Particularly to wear during visits to defecation grounds
4. Water supply and water carrying	
Containers for carrying water	Containers should be easy to keep clean, should be glazed if of pottery, and should not have rims under which dirt can collect
Containers with lids for storing water	
Carts for carrying larger water containers	
Adequate fuel for boiling water	
Household water filters	
5. Food hygiene	
Adequate fuel for cooking	
Means of storing food above ground	
Means of covering food	

concentrate on only a limited range of improvements, so not everything listed in Table 5 will be needed.

Promoting soap and shoes

Because of the crucial importance of regular hand washing, soap may be the material most urgently needed. In most rural areas it is already available, but is often too costly to be used very often. In West Bengal villages, 'soap is used mainly by people who have relatives working in a town, though most people have some for washing their hair' (SDC 180).

It may be possible for project organizers to secure an improved supply by making purchases of commercially-produced soap themselves, taking advantage of the reduced price available with a bulk purchase. However, soap can be made from materials which are widely available — typically from soda ash, lime, and an oil or fat (e.g. palm oil). It can be made on a domestic scale, or developed as a small industry (see the leaflet "Preparation of Soap" listed in the bibliography).

In places where hookworm is a problem, the wearing of shoes is always a useful precaution. But shoes are usually too expensive unless there is somebody locally who makes them, or unless this trade can be introduced. Thus, the technical assistance needed in support of improved hygiene might include efforts to promote the making of shoes or sandals as well as soap.

Fuel for cooking

Fuel for cooking is an important consideration because the thorough cooking of meat may be a necessary precaution against tapeworm; fish may need lengthy cooking as a precaution against other parasitic worms; and the boiling of all drinking water may be advisable. In many areas, however, firewood has become a very scarce commodity, and this may be the most difficult of all material deficiencies to overcome. In such circumstances, a long-term solution could be the establishment of plantations for the systematic production of firewood. The introduction of more efficient stoves can be another useful step, and the very compact charcoal stove in Fig.5 should be noted.

Water filters

In some instances where firewood is too scarce to allow for the boiling of drinking water, and where there is little prospect of improving the community's water supply, it may help to provide families with household water filters. For example, this was done by one project in Brazil which aimed to improve housing and sanitation simultaneously (BRZ 101). Filters are also items which can be made locally, either by a potter, or by improvisation from cans or oil-drums. Whatever container is used, it should be filled with clean sand, the type that may be obtained from a river bed, and it must have a hole at the bottom through which the filtered water may emerge. Used intermittently in a household, such filters will not remove bacteriological infections from the water, but can be a very useful precaution in areas where diseases such as guineaworm and bilharzia are prevalent. Further

food
storage
basket

charcoal
pot stove

drum for
water storage

Fig.5. Cooking in West Africa. Positive factors for food hygiene include the hanging storage basket and the compact, efficient pot stove. Negative factors include the lack of covers on stored foods, and the way that some pots are kept on the ground. (See 'New design for a kitchen in Ghana', Appropriate Technology, Volume 1 (2), *1974, pp.20-1.)*

details, with some discussion of other types of filter, are given in the booklet by Cairncross and Feachem listed in the bibliography.

Clean water

Using household filters or boiling water is not, of course, the best response to a polluted water supply. It will be far more satisfactory to provide an adequate supply of reliably clean water. One approach will be to help individual households to obtain clean water by collecting it from roofs, or by protecting their backyard wells. More often, though, the most relevant measures will be to construct a community water supply by protecting village wells and springs, or by building a piped supply, perhaps with a slow sand filter. Again, the booklet by Cairncross and Feachem gives more detail.

Food hygiene

Food hygiene is one of the most important subjects which has to be dealt with in health education, and this depends on a range of material factors, including fuel for cooking, and availability of clean water. If shortages of fuel present problems, recipes may need to be developed to give the maximum protection of health for the minimum use of fuel. Eating raw vegetables as a salad can be dangerous in areas with poor sanitation. Salad vegetables may not be washed well where water supplies are inadequate, and could carry parasitic worm infections from the soil. Even where water is available to wash them, it may be water that is unfit to drink. Quick cooking methods such as parboiling and frying can be used with many salad vegetables. Such methods conserve the vitamin content of the food and use little fuel, but at the same time overcome most of the hygiene problems.

Food storage

Food hygiene also depends on the adequacy of food storage arrangements in the home. One basic requirement is that it should be possible to store food above ground level. This can only be done if there are shelves or tables or some other storage arrangements in the kitchen, and the provision of these where they are lacking might be another aspect of technical assistance for better hygiene. One device used in some African countries is the hanging storage basket (Fig.5), which is likely to defeat the intrusion even of rats. All cooked food, and all meat and fish, should be covered to prevent access by flies, even if it is to be kept only an hour or two.

Bad food hygiene and unwashed hands are the means by which many excreta-related diseases are most readily spread, so these two subjects need to be emphasized in all sanitation projects, whether or not latrines are built. With both subjects, simple practical help with materials such as soap, or with water supplies, or with cooking utensils may be the best form of technical assistance.

Paying for better sanitation

Many of the basic materials required for improvements in hygiene are inexpensive. However, better kitchen equipment and household water filters may be too costly for many families, and so may latrines and better water supplies. Projects can very often plan to minimize these costs by using local materials and products, or by introducing latrines or kitchen improvements that householders can construct for themselves. There are still, however, some improvements which demand the use of cement or corrugated iron, or manufactured equipment. Although project organizers can sometimes minimize costs by making bulk purchases, or even arranging a subsidy on some items, there may still be a considerable sum which the villagers themselves must raise.

Savings clubs

There are several ways in which such financial burdens may be eased. For example, a savings club might be organized whereby families save up for the desired improvement over a period of, say, a year. Savings clubs of this type hold a weekly meeting for members at which time they pay a fixed contribution and have a stamp stuck on their cards. When sufficient money has been accumulated, the materials which club members have agreed to buy are purchased in bulk and shared among the members of the club. This system has been successfully used in Zambia for the purchase of corrugated iron for home improvements, but unless interest in the ultimate objective is very strong, it is unlikely to work well.

Revolving loan schemes

For this reason, latrines have more often been financed through revolving loan schemes so that the desired improvement comes much sooner, and repayments are made when the benefits of the project are apparent. Under this system, the agency responsible for the sanitation work sets aside a fixed sum of money from which the loans to householders are made. As individuals pay back the money that has been lent to them, it becomes available to other people in the same community. The people should be encouraged to regard these loan funds as money belonging to the community as a whole and not to an impersonal body such as a bank. They will then be aware that delaying repayment of their loan will postpone the day when a neighbour can borrow money for his own latrine or other improvement.

The problem with using revolving loan funds to pay for sanitary improvements is that a latrine or a water tank does not generate extra income for the household from which the loan can be repaid. Loan schemes have mainly been successful where the building of latrines has been part of a wider programme which includes income-generating activities as well.

A revolving fund in Kerala, India

In a fishing community on the Kerala coast of India (KER 17), the establishment of a revolving fund for latrines was one of several projects undertaken with a successful fishing co-operative. Along with other activities, women attended adult literacy classes, took their children to a clinic, and were taught about the health hazards associated with defecating in the open. When they attended this local clinic, the women used a latrine, and gradually took to the idea of having one of their own at home. Pit latrines with a water-seal pan and brick privy hut were proposed, costing 750 rupees to build (in 1975). If a family raised 250 rupees, the remainder was loaned from the revolving fund; the householder then repaid the loan at the rate of 15 rupees per month.

Revolving loans in Cabrobo, Brazil

Revolving loan funds have also worked well in Brazil, where community development workers have encouraged people in poor suburbs to build their own pit latrines. In one instance, two Peace Corps volunteers helped launch a campaign on the fringes of the small town of Cabrobo (BRZ 147). At public meetings, the men discussed the technical aspects of installation and maintenance, and the women were taught about disease prevention and the need for latrines. This was followed up by home visits, film shows on health matters, and small weekly collections made towards the latrine fund. Once one family had paid a fixed proportion of the total cost, a group of families joined together to help them dig the latrine pit and line it with bricks. Prefabricated concrete floor-slabs were then provided and installed by a mason.

Extension work and technical assistance

In projects that involve the construction of latrines or water supply equipment, the problems of materials and money are sometimes less significant than those of skills and maintenance. A badly-constructed or badly-maintained latrine may create far more serious sanitary conditions than existed before it was built.

Assisting with construction

Several ways of providing assistance with skilled construction work have been tried out. On some projects the design of latrines has been modified so that all the construction can be undertaken with skills that already exist in the village. In other instances, technicians have been employed to carry out the skilled part of each job. Sometimes these technicians will merely act as contractors and do the job *for* the villagers. Occasionally, however, they may function as extension workers, teaching some of their skills to the people in the course of doing the job, thereby working *with* the villagers.

Two kinds of practical help which a sanitation project may need to offer to villagers have already been mentioned: supplies of materials, and loans with money. Help with skills which the community lacks is a third kind of aid which may be needed. One should regard these three complementary ways of helping rural people as three essential aspects of village-level technical assistance.

A large part of planning a programme will consist of working out how these different kinds of assistance are to be provided. However, little information is provided on this subject in manuals on sanitation, and most literature on appropriate technology concentrates on equipment, without much discussion of the technical assistance that will be needed if the equipment is to go into widespread use. It is often thought to be sufficient to set up a workshop or training centre where equipment can be made and demonstrated. But real village-level technical assistance programmes, with technicians working in the local community, are rarely attempted.

The point applies as much to agriculture as to sanitation. In 1975, a brief survey of agricultural projects supported by Oxfam in Tanzania revealed much interest in appropriate technology. In some places, this had inspired the design of new farm implements and new equipment for poultry-keeping. Although efforts were being made to persuade people to try out this equipment by demonstrating it to them, there was no active extension work or technical assistance in the villages, and so little of the equipment went into regular use.

Technical assistance in Zimbabwe

The only really good example of village-level technical assistance that the author was able to find in a sanitation-related subject was in Zimbabwe (RHO 10). There, a significant number of people have houses with corrugated iron roofs. The tanks which collect water from these roofs provide a cleaner drinking water supply than is otherwise available. Metal tanks can be purchased, but are expensive and suffer from corrosion problems unless installed with very great care. However, staff at a rural training centre perfected the construction of a cheaper and more durable tank made of ferrocement (Figs 6 and 7). The method used for making these tanks has been fully described by Simon Watt (in Chapter 7 of his book, which is noted in the bibliography). What is of particular interest here is the system of technical assistance which was devised so that householders could acquire the tanks. A builder was trained to construct them, and he then worked alongside any house-holder who wanted a tank for the four or five days needed to complete it.

This was not a self-help arrangement, where the householder was expected to complete the job on his own, but neither was it a case of the householder calling in the builder to do the whole job for him. He had to work *with* the builder, and could be expected to learn a good deal in the process about the use of cement, and fixing gutters and downpipes. This system of technical assistance worked very successfully for two years during which some 200 tanks were built in the villages. Then increases in the price of cement made the tanks too expensive for the villagers, and work slowed down.

Fig.6. Detail of ferrocement water tanks near Bulawayo, Zimbabwe. The picture shows the guttering, down-pipes, and the sheet metal cover on each tank. For a more general view, see Fig.7. (Photo: Arnold Pacey.)

Vegetable-growing

Another example of village-level technical assistance was given in a previous booklet in this series, 'Gardening for Better Nutrition'. In this instance, a vegetable-growing project employed a skilled gardener to work with housewives and mothers, helping them to start gardens, erect fences and do the initial heavy digging. This practical help was given, not just as a service, but as part of the educational or extension process. One problem was that barbed wire had to be supplied for the fences. Householders were expected to pay the full price for this, but there was a loan scheme to help with the payment, and costs were subsidized for the very poor.

This project is particularly worthy of note because it includes all three of the different kinds of practical help which may be necessary in technical assistance — help with materials, finance and skills.

Technical assistance for latrine construction

There are many kinds of toilet or privy which can be built in rural sanitation projects, but by far the simplest and most widely used is the pit latrine. This will be taken here as an example to illustrate how village-level technical assistance may be arranged in projects where latrines are built.

Fig. 7. Ferrocement water tanks near Bulawayo, Zimbabwe. The tanks collect water from the roofs of these low-cost houses at a rural training centre, and are designed to be built by a trained technician working alongside the householder. (Photo: Arnold Pacey.)

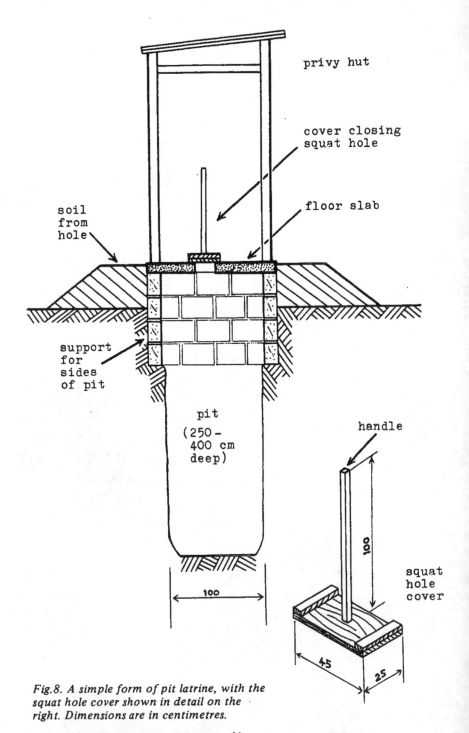

privy hut

cover closing
squat hole

floor slab

soil
from
hole

support
for
sides
of pit

pit
(250 –
400 cm
deep)

100

handle

100

squat
hole
cover

45

25

Fig.8. A simple form of pit latrine, with the squat hole cover shown in detail on the right. Dimensions are in centimetres.

41

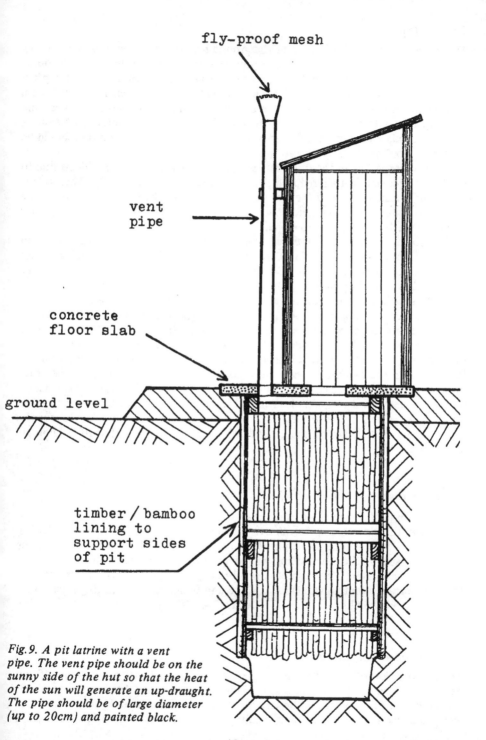

fly-proof mesh

vent pipe

concrete floor slab

ground level

timber / bamboo lining to support sides of pit

Fig. 9. A pit latrine with a vent pipe. The vent pipe should be on the sunny side of the hut so that the heat of the sun will generate an up-draught. The pipe should be of large diameter (up to 20cm) and painted black.

42

The pit latrine

The pit latrine consists of a hole in the ground bridged by a floor slab or squatting plate, around which is built a hut to provide privacy (Fig.8). In most developing countries, people squat to defecate, so usually all that is needed inside the privy hut is a hole in the floor slab and not a raised seat. There is often also a cover with a long handle, enabling the hole to be closed when not in use to prevent flies from entering. It should be remembered that flies which have made contact with excreta can play a major part in transferring infection to food, and every effort should be made to keep them from getting to the excreta in the first place.

Ample ventilation in the privy hut is obviously desirable, and problems due to smell and flies are further reduced if a vent pipe is installed (Fig.9). When this is placed on the sunny side of the hut and painted black, the heat of the sun on the pipe will create an up-draught, drawing air from the pit, and trapping any flies under the mesh at the top of the pipe.

The construction of pit latrines requires less expertise than other sanitation techniques, but most householders will require some skilled help in digging the pit and constructing the floor slab. Digging the pit is a straightforward if laborious job. Families can often work together, helping each other. It is often recommended that pits should be 4 metres deep and 1 metre square, but inexperienced people should not usually dig pits more than 2 metres (or 7 feet) deep because of the danger that a collapse of the sides could bury them. In some conditions, a circular pit will be less likely to collapse than a square one. Timber supports or other shoring can be used to protect diggers, and it may be a good idea to train one or two people in each village to shore up the sides of pits as they are dug. The other problem is that people are generally not accustomed to following plans and measurements, and may tend to make the top of the pit too wide to be bridged by a floor slab. In St. Lucia (West Indies), one way of solving this has been to supply a wooden frame to place on the ground, which provides the outline of the hole to be dug (SDC 105).

Requirements for technical assistance

Another point at which skilled help may be needed is in lining the completed pit to prevent the sides crumbling and to provide a foundation for the floor slab. In very stable clay soils it might be possible to confine the lining to the top part of the pit. More usually, though, a lining will be needed throughout the whole depth of the pit, using timber, corrugated iron, bricks, concrete blocks or ferrocement (cement plastered on to a wire mesh). Figs 8 and 9 illustrate contrasting types of pit lining (concrete blocks and timbers) extending to different depths.

Construction and maintenance

The construction of floor slabs is a bigger problem, and the type and design of slab has to be carefully matched to the kind of technical assistance that can be organized. The privy hut may sometimes be left for the householder to build according to his own taste. However, if there is difficulty in obtaining suitable materials locally,

43

or if a vent pipe is to be installed, assistance may be required at this stage too.

Rural latrines should generally be built by and for individual households. Members of the household will then be responsible for cleaning and maintenance, tasks which are often badly neglected in communal facilities. Even when households own their individual latrines, however, cleaning is often insufficiently thorough, and one of the tasks of village workers dealing with sanitation should be to visit homes to talk about the importance of cleanliness, and check on the state of the latrine.

It may be seen from these details that the planning and organization of technical assistance, even for a simple latrine, presents several crucial problems. Recent work in rural communities illustrates four main ways in which this technical assistance can be arranged, as follows:

1. Village health workers may be trained to advise householders on more difficult tasks.
2. Health professionals may supervise the work.
3. Building technicians may work with the householders in constructing the latrines.
4. Components that are difficult to make may be manufactured in a central 'factory' and distributed to householders.

Technical assistance from village health workers

Where village health workers provide most of the necessary technical assistance, it is usually important that latrines should be of very simple design, and constructed, preferably, with local materials. This may mean using timber or bamboo extensively, which is only feasible where there is timber available of a reasonably termite-proof kind. When this approach is adopted, floor slabs are frequently built up of compacted earth on a timber framework. Health experts frown on this practice because of the difficulty of keeping an earth floor adequately clean. However, some communities do have traditional ways of making an earth floor smooth and waterproof, and there is need for more research into these methods (see Chapter 4).

Technical assistance from health professionals

Health professionals supervising latrine construction will have had far more training than the village health workers, but will not be technicians. Often, therefore, professionals need special additional training if they are to be involved in latrine construction. Such people have included public health inspectors in Nigeria (SDC 94), and health assistants in Zimbabwe (SDC 102). In both these countries, villagers make their latrine floor slabs of reinforced concrete. This entails using a mould into which the concrete is poured and allowed to set. In Zimbabwe the mould is made of wood, and is frequently improvised on the site under the supervision of the health assistant, but in Nigeria, steel moulds are loaned to the communities where latrines are being built. The loan of the moulds thus forms an additional element in the technical assistance package.

Building technicians

Building technicians who work alongside villagers to construct latrines can show them what needs to be done rather than just instructing or advising them. This approach has not often been applied in latrine building, but its potential is illustrated by the project previously described, in which people were helped to build water tanks.

Factories

The 'factory' approach to latrine projects involves supplying householders with ready-made floor slabs, and sometimes with prefabricated privy huts also (BRZ 147). Usually, a central depot is set up where floor slabs are manufactured for a group of villages. Individual householders dig their own latrine pits, the floor slabs are then delivered to them and they are often given help with installation, too. In Somalia, Oxfam funds paid for the manufacture of 4200 floor slabs in a project of this kind (SOM 10). In some of the communities aided, every household acquired a latrine, although in other villages, only a quarter of the households co-operated. The cost of the floor slabs was at first US$5.00 each, but with the rise in cement prices during 1974, this figure doubled, and efforts were made to manage with a smaller slab.

In St. Lucia (West Indies), it has also been found best to manufacture floor slabs at a central site (SDC 105). This leads to a better product as quality control is easier, although the transport of slabs to the site can present problems.

Advantages of ready-made slabs

Providing householders with complete slabs can solve the biggest construction problem they face in building a pit latrine, and can make it more feasible for every home to have its own privy. Providing ready-made slabs also opens up the possibility of introducing new types made of glass fibre or PVC plastic. These materials give a smoother surface which is easier to clean than concrete, but their cost is still prohibitive, and their use confined mainly to emergency applications.

Conclusion

These different ways of organizing latrine construction between them give a very clear picture of what is involved in village-level technical assistance. In almost every instance, the supply of materials has to be arranged. This may be a small amount of cement, or it may be a completed slab. Where costly items have to be supplied, the arrangements for technical assistance may also have to include help with finance, perhaps through a loan scheme. Then there is the question of skills which must either be provided or imparted. Sometimes this important aspect of technical assistance will be arranged by offering instruction, advice and supervision. At other times, however, it will be achieved by lending the services of a trained technician to each householder in turn. Either way, the planning of this aspect of the project is likely to be crucial for its long-term success.

4. Approaches to Latrine Design

Available types of latrine

Several times in this booklet it has been stated that latrines may not always be practicable or even relevant to the sanitary needs of rural communities. It is necessary now to emphasize that there are many circumstances in which latrines are vitally relevant, and where rural householders ought to be positively encouraged to acquire their own. Latrines are likely to be most practicable where people are rebuilding and modernising their houses and can afford privies good enough to benefit health unambiguously. They are likely to be most urgently relevant in larger villages, and in places where population density is rising fast. In such circumstances, there may be no other way of alleviating serious public health problems except by building latrines. Then, if people are too poor to pay for their own, some kind of subsidy may well be justified. However, if latrines are subsidized in this way, the best results are likely to be achieved if related improvements in housing can be included in the project, because latrines which are unrelated to the home environment are often misused. In places where household privies are not yet feasible, one possibility would be to build latrines at schools.

How to choose

Whichever of these circumstances prompts the building of latrines, the question must be tackled: what type will be best? The need will usually be for equipment that is simple to assemble, does not depend on specialized imported components, and is low in cost. Also, the servicing and maintenance of the latrine should be relatively easy for local people to organize. Among the types of latrine which are likely to fit these requirements are composting and pit latrines, bucket latrines, and aqua-privies.

Pit latrines

These are the cheapest and simplest of the options to construct, and apart from the need for regular cleaning, make few demands on users. However, they can only be built where the soil does not become waterlogged, and where a pit can be dug down to a depth of at least 2.0 to 2.5 metres. The simplest types of pit latrine are also limited in application because of problems with smell and with flies. These difficulties can be overcome by installing a vent pipe (Fig.9), or by using a water-seal pan, such as that favoured in India (Fig.10).

In places where the soil is free from stones, a different version of the pit latrine can be made using a manually-operated auger to bore a deep hole in the ground. A hole 25 centimetres in diameter and at least 5 metres deep is required, and can usually be bored with an auger more quickly than a pit can be dug. Where bored-hole latrines of this type are to be constructed, the loan of augers to villagers will obviously be a necessary form of technical assistance.

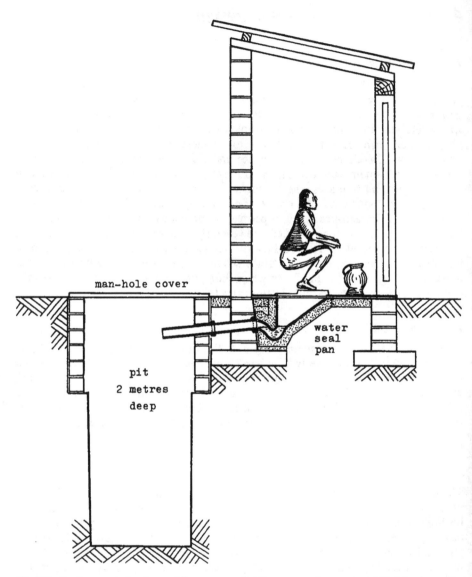

man-hole cover

pit
2 metres
deep

water
seal
pan

Fig.10. Soakage pit latrine with water seal. The user takes water with him into the latrine for anal cleaning and to flush the pan.

Bucket latrines

If soil conditions do not allow the building of pit latrines, the remaining choice for a rural community is likely to be between bucket latrines, composting latrines, and aqua-privies. All these require more organization and discipline for successful operation than does the pit latrine. Regular cleaning is, of course, essential with all types of latrine, but good organization is particularly necessary with bucket latrines to ensure that they are emptied regularly (usually daily), and to see that this is done in a hygienic manner. Because of the difficulty of achieving this, bucket latrines should only be introduced in exceptional circumstances. Composting latrines and aqua-privies also need to be emptied periodically, though at intervals of months rather than days, and both types can be attractive options in many respects.

Aqua-privies

The aqua-privy is strongly favoured for rural sanitation in a number of countries. It works on a system whereby excreta decomposes in a tank of water beneath the latrine floor-slab (Fig.11). Excess liquid leaves this tank via an overflow pipe and a soakaway in the ground. To avoid smell and ensure correct operation, the water surface in the tank must be maintained at the maximum level allowed by the overflow. For this purpose, it is usually necessary for about one bucket of water to be poured into the tank each day through the squat hole. In places where people use water for cleaning themselves after defecation, sufficient water is added as a matter of course. However, where people use toilet paper or other solid matter for anal cleaning, the water has to be added separately. This requires more organization, especially where the water has to be carried some distance, so this is a task which is often neglected. It is not surprising, therefore, that in general, aqua-privies are most successful where anal cleaning is done with water.

One other point about aqua-privies is that a residual sludge forms in them which must be cleared out at intervals of, typically, a year. This is another task that is frequently neglected, with the result that many aqua-privies give two or three years of good service, and then begin to cause dangerous pollution problems by overflowing. The usual reason why desludging of these privies is neglected is the *lack of effective organization* to ensure regular servicing. But another factor is that desludging is difficult to undertake without specialized equipment. The latter problem is avoided in a new type of aqua-privy which can be desludged by gravity flow.

A confusing variety of names is used to describe aqua-privies. In Africa, any type of privy is likely to be called a WC (water closet). In India, however, the term 'septic tank' is commonly applied to pit latrines with water-seal pans (as Fig.10) and to aqua-privies also. This can be highly misleading, because in international usage, the term 'septic tank' is reserved for a more elaborate arrangement whereby a flush latrine discharges into a tank. Such devices are far too costly to be considered here.

Composting latrines

A quite different approach is provided by composting latrines, which deal with excreta in a dry state. Besides excreta they need to be regularly fed with vegetable matter, food wastes, and sometimes with wood ashes. When operated correctly, these latrines convert the mixture of materials into a safe, sweet-smelling compost that can be used on land without any hazard to health. The compost will take a certain time to form: as little as three months with one type of composting latrine, or over a year with another. The need to put vegetable matter into the composting compartment means one extra task that has to be organized, but a community's output of crop wastes sometimes matches this requirement reasonably well.

A great many different types of composting latrine have been designed and used, and it is not possible to describe a 'typical' example. With the sole exception of Vietnam, there is no country where these latrines have been in regular use for any length of time. Despite the lack of practical experience in operating them, however, the principle of the composting latrine seems very promising; interested readers should try the books by Rybzinski and McMichael which are listed in the bibliography.

Composting in pit latrines

Where pit latrines are in use, they can also be adapted to make compost, and have

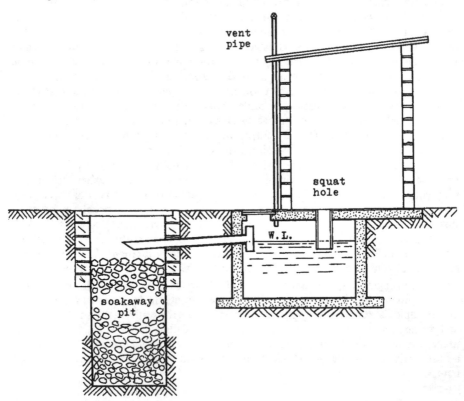

Fig.11. The principle of the aqua-privy. The water level in the tank needs to be kept at the level marked 'W.L.' by adding water daily. Many kinds of soakaway are possible to deal with water overflowing from the tank. The soakaway shown consists of a pit filled with broken stones.

been especially designed for this purpose in Bangladesh. Sanitation workers there recommend that, when the pit has been dug, a thick layer of grass and other vegetable matter should be placed at the bottom (Fig.14). As the latrine is used, further vegetable matter should be added. Finally, when the pit is nearly full, a new latrine should be made and the original pit sealed with a layer of soil. After a period of six months or more, the compost may be safely dug out and used on the land.

Choosing latrines for a rural situation

Among the factors which should influence the choice of a particular type of latrine for a rural community are: cost; potential for fostering better hygiene; and the kind of technical assistance needed to erect them. Some details of these criteria are summarized in Table 6, but there is one other important point to consider. The latrines must be of such a kind that when the 'project' ends and the sanitation experts depart, people will go on using, maintaining, and when necessary, replacing them. This means that the social discipline and organization needed to operate the latrines must be compatible with other kinds of organization in the family and community. This applies particularly to topping up aqua-privies with water and adding vegetable material to composting latrines. These tasks, and the regular cleaning of any latrine, must become part of the daily routine of specific members of each family. Where family organization does not make this possible, the latrine is not likely to be of long-term benefit.

Arranging construction

Another aspect of local organization is the way in which building work is arranged, because this affects the ultimate replacement of latrines when this is necessary, and the construction of new ones when new houses are built. In places where people build their own houses using their own labour, the latrines must be capable of being built the same way. Where, however, there are specialized building craftsmen who contract for the construction of houses, then the latrines should be within *their* capabilities.

Because pit latrines are the simplest type to build and operate, they are likely to be used in preference to other types in many programmes. However, where soils are very shallow, pit latrines cannot normally be built, and on waterlogged land, neither pit latrines nor aqua-privies are suitable. Construction of pit latrines will also be difficult in very sandy soils because the sides of every pit will need to be shored up while the pit is being dug and after completion.

Materials and costs

Another factor affecting the type of latrine to choose is the availability of materials, and related to this, the question of costs. With the possible exception of the floor slab, pit latrines can often be built entirely of local materials. Aqua-privies, which typically cost at least twice as much as pit latrines, incorporate a tank which must be completely watertight, and which is most often built of reinforced concrete. With aqua-privies, then, there is little scope for using local materials. Composting

50

latrines, however, have compartments which hold relatively dry wastes, to which no water is added, and they can be built from a wide variety of materials. In Vietnam, for example, compacted clay, sun-dried bricks, fired bricks, and concrete have all been used (SDC 113). There is so far little experience of the cost of building composting latrines, but local materials should make them cheaper than aqua-privies.

Level of technical assistance

The availability of technical assistance ought to influence the choice between different types of privy because pit and bucket latrines are the only types that one can reasonably expect unskilled people to build. Even then, it is best if a village health worker with relevant training can be on hand to advise and help. Aqua-privies and most composting latrines require the services of a skilled builder, and it would be useful for householders to work alongside the builder, as suggested in the previous chapter. Alternatively, the builder could be wholly responsible for construction up to the level of the floor slab, and the householder could then be left to build the privy hut. Another problem which may arise where aqua-privies or composting latrines are being built is that their relatively high cost may make some kind of revolving loan scheme necessary to help people with the financial burden.

It is most important, then, that the planning of the technical assistance programme is closely related to the design of the latrines. In many projects, shortages of funds or of skilled manpower will greatly restrict technical assistance, and so reduce the choice to the simplest types of latrine.

Consideration of housing conditions

A knowledge of local housing conditions should be an important influence when making decisions about choosing a privy. It has already been suggested that the cost of a latrine ought not to exceed 10 per cent of the cost of building a house. The layout of the house is also important because most of the latrines discussed are best located some distance from the dwelling, in a backyard or garden. It is usually recommended that pit latrines should be at least 6 metres from the house, which is the type of spacing indicated in Figs 2 and 3.

Establishing the purpose of latrines

One point which may need to be considered is whether everybody is agreed about the purpose of the latrines. It is easy to take for granted that when privies are installed, it is to promote cleanliness and protect health. But as mentioned in Chapter 2, many people will be looking for more general improvements in their standard of living, and may see the purpose of the latrines purely in terms of convenience and general amenity. If one is not interested in this aspect, then insufficient weight may be given to the kind of detail which will most strongly influence local attitudes to the project.

Maintaining traditions of fertilizer use

Perhaps the greatest problem of this sort will arise in areas which already have a long tradition of using latrines. Sometimes, the main purpose is to gain some privacy for defecation, a particular priority in crowded conditions. More important, though, are the traditional latrines (already mentioned) which exist, mainly in Asia, to collect excreta for use as fertilizer. Before the revolution in 1949, peasants in China were compelled to defecate in their landlord's latrine, not for the good of their health, but for the benefit of his crops. Today, in some parts of Asia, latrines are still built over fishponds as a way of fertilizing them, and the contents of bucket latrines are carried away for application to the land.

Where these practices exist, any new and more hygienic latrine that is introduced must produce fertilizer if it is to be acceptable. A latrine which protects health by causing excreta to disappear for ever into an impossibly deep pit or into a sewer does not fulfil the purpose which people expect of it. The success of composting latrines in Vietnam has undoubtedly come about because they were promoted as a means of producing fertilizer. Agricultural trials were undertaken which showed that the hygienic compost from the latrines actually produced better crops than raw excreta, and the results of these trials were printed in the handbook used by health workers (SDC 113).

Compost heaps

Where composting latrines cannot be used, an alternative is to introduce bucket latrines with arrangements for emptying their contents on to a compost heap. If this method is adopted, the compost heap must be carefully managed, with vegetable matter as well as excreta added to the pile so that the material decomposes thoroughly. If this is done properly, the compost heap will generate heat with temperatures of 55-65°C which will kill any parasite eggs in a few days.

Holding tanks

Another method of excreta treatment, for use where people need fertilizer for fish ponds, is to store the excreta in a holding tank for 24 hours before releasing it into the pond, adding a little ammonium sulphate to the tank. However, this method may adversely affect some species of fish, and is therefore of restricted use.

Improving existing latrines

In some circumstances where a traditional type of latrine is in use, but is unsatisfactory from a health point of view, sanitary engineers should consider whether it might be more acceptable to improve the existing latrine rather than introduce a new type. For example, where bucket latrines already exist, as they often do in India, sanitation workers have frequently attempted to improve them.

Checking improvements in hygiene

This brings us back to one of the most crucial points that should influence a choice of latrine: does it make possible a significant improvement in hygiene? No latrine *automatically* creates better sanitary conditions, because good sanitation depends more on people's habits and discipline than on equipment. The purpose of a latrine, from the health point of view, is simply *to make good hygiene easier.* Most types of privy discussed in the last few pages can do this, provided that they are well constructed, with smooth floors which are easy to clean, and with adequate precautions to exclude flies. However, bucket latrines and simple pit latrines are often very inadequate in these respects.

The problem with simple pit latrines without a vent pipe is that flies may gain access to the excreta and may spread infection by later getting into somebody's house and walking over food stored there. Access to excreta by flies can be stopped by placing a cover over the squat hole when the latrine is not in use. Another problem with simple latrines arises when they have earthen floors which cannot be thoroughly cleaned. There is some danger, then, that very basic types of latrine may actually make good hygiene *more* difficult than if no latrine were built at all. This is one of the reasons why one should be cautious about introducing low-cost latrines to rural communities. There may be a few communities that are better off without them.

To sum up, then, the criteria to use in deciding on the kind of latrines which might be most appropriate for a specific community should include soil conditions, costs, technical assistance, housing conditions, anal cleaning methods, potential for better hygiene, and sometimes requirements for fertilizer. The more important of these factors are summarized in Table 6, which is adapted from a booklet by Feachem and Cairncross (1978) that gives additional technical information about the different types of latrine.

The construction of the floor slab

One technical problem which is common to most types of latrine is the design and construction of the floor slab. As indicated in the previous chapter, the floor slab may be the only part of constructing a pit latrine which calls for any engineering skill. It may thus be the focus of the technical assistance programme, and hence the focus of relationships between sanitation engineers and local people.

Health is also at issue because a dirty floor slab may harbour roundworm *(Ascaris)* eggs and hookworm larvae. Of course, cleanliness depends very much on the people using the privy, but a smooth, hard, impermeable floor lends itself to easy cleaning. On a rough and porous floor, by contrast, hookworm and roundworm infection may persist even after the most thorough brushing and washing.

Ease of cleaning is also important in enhancing the acceptability of the latrine to users. A dirty latrine is as unpleasant as it is dangerous to health, and a latrine which demands a time-consuming routine for cleaning is not likely to be popular with whoever is expected to do this job.

The squat hole versus the seat

Another issue affecting social acceptability is whether the floor slab has the usual squat hole, or whether there is a raised seat in the western style. Although the squat hole is very widespread, people in some parts of Africa and the Caribbean are increasingly expressing a preference for the raised seat. In the latter region, where both types of latrine co-exist, 'a higher standard of living is associated with the "sit-down" toilet' (SDC 105). Advantages claimed for it are that it is easier on pregnant women and old people, who find squatting difficult, and that it is less often fouled. However, certain cultural and religious groups still insist on a squat hole.

Table 6. Some criteria for the appropriateness of different types of latrine.

LATRINE	Cost to build	Depth of soil needed	Potential for better hygiene	Technical assistance needed	Best anal cleaning material	Fertilizer production
Simple pit latrine (Fig.8)	low	deep soil, not water-logged	medium	simple: mainly with floor slab	any	can do
Pit latrine with vent pipe (Fig.9)	low	deep soil, not water-logged	good	simple: vent pipe to be supplied	any	not easily
Soakage pit latrine, water-seal (Fig.10)	high	deep soil, not water-logged	good	skilled builder needed	water	no
Aqua-privy (Fig.11)	high	not water-logged	good	skilled builder needed	water	no
Composting latrine	moderate	any	good	skilled builder needed	paper	yes
Bucket latrine	low	any	poor	simple	any	can do

Since floor slabs with squat holes predominate, it is these that will be considered. As explained in the previous chapter, they are usually made of reinforced concrete. This is not the ideal material, because its rough surface is difficult to clean. However, by plastering the completed slab with a very wet cement mix, a smoother surface can be made.

Construction of the slab

The quality of the slab will depend on the mould used for casting the concrete. The best results are obtained by casting slabs face downwards in a steel mould, and carefully inverting the mould to tip out the slab when the concrete has set. The mould should be shaped to make the finished slab slope downwards to the squat hole, with two flat, slightly raised foot-rests (Fig.12). Placed on either side of the

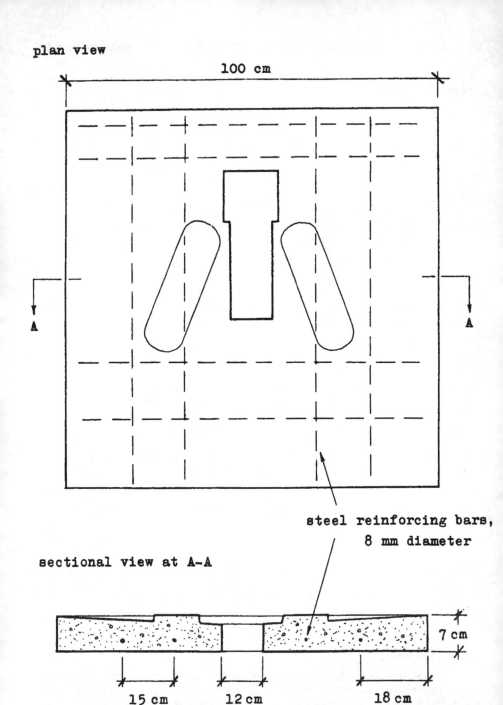

plan view

100 cm

steel reinforcing bars,
8 mm diameter

sectional view at A-A

7 cm

15 cm   12 cm   18 cm

Fig.12. A simple concrete floor slab, showing a typical arrangement of the steel reinforcing bars and the layout of squat hole and foot rests.

hole, the foot-rests help people to squat exactly in the right place to allow their faeces to drop through into the pit. If the remainder of the floor surface slopes slightly, this makes it easier to rinse down the slab, and ensures that spilt water and urine drain into the pit. If the finished latrine is to have a vent pipe, the hole through which it will pass must also be cast into the floor slab.

Where steel moulds are not available and an improvised wood mould is used, the slab will more often be cast face up, and the mould partly dismantled before the

plan view

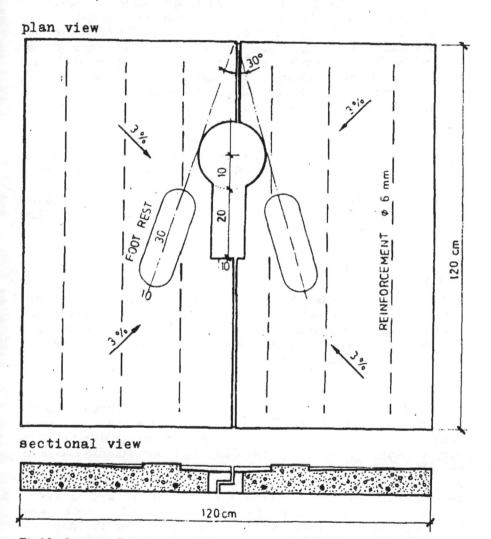

sectional view

Fig.13. Concrete floor slab used in Nigeria, showing how it is made in two parts for easier handling. The slab has a 3 per cent slope from each corner towards the squat hole. Dimensions are in centimetres. Dashed lines show the positions of the reinforcing bars. (By courtesy of John Wiley & Sons.)

slab is lifted out. The floor surface will then be flat, and the foot-rests will have to be built up in a separate operation.

With either type of mould, the slab should be reinforced with steel rods of about 8 mm in diameter, spaced as shown in Fig.12. These should be embedded in the concrete, preferably nearer the bottom surface than the top, and should nowhere be exposed. The way to achieve this, when casting a slab face up, is first to place concrete in the mould to an even depth of about 2.5 cm (one inch). Next, lay the reinforcing rods carefully into position before placing the rest of the concrete. The finished slab should be 6 to 7 cm thick, and will typically be a metre square.

This type of slab will weigh 150 kilograms, and will thus be difficult to move into place over the pit; clumsy handling is not easy to avoid, and may lead to the slab cracking. The problem will be especially acute if slabs are cast at a central depot and then delivered to individual households. One project in Nigeria (SDC 94) has therefore used steel moulds which allow slabs to be cast in two halves (Fig.13) thus making them lighter and easier to lift.

Size of squat hole

The diagrams illustrate suitable dimensions for the squat hole. If the hole is much smaller than indicated, the slab will be fouled rather often, but if it is bigger, it could prove a danger to children. One reason why children do not use latrines regularly is said to be that they are frightened by the hole. This is a problem that village health workers could investigate; they could also experiment by making some latrines with two squat holes, one of a smaller size for children.

Earthen floor slabs

A floor of damp soil in a latrine can easily become infected with hookworm larvae, and therefore the use of earthen floors in latrines should, if possible, be avoided. However, there are many sanitation projects with limited resources where concrete floor slabs are not feasible. In these instances floors with an earthen surface supported on timber beams are very widely used.

Construction

The normal method of construction is to build up a sturdy platform of termite-proof timber or bamboo to span the top of the latrine pit. Next, sacking or a layer of leaves or grass is laid across the platform, leaving a hole in the middle, and a thick layer of compacted earth is laid on top of that. Fig.14 shows the first stage in this kind of construction as illustrated by an instruction booklet written in Bangladesh. A comparable booklet used by the builders of composting latrines in Vietnam describes a very similar bamboo frame, specifying that the oldest parts of the bamboo should be used. To prolong their life, the bamboo poles should be soaked in lime water for at least a week before the start of construction. The poles should be long enough for a good deal of their length to be supported on the ground at either side of the pit, where they should be carefully bedded in a layer of damp clay. The Vietnamese booklet then instructs the builder to spread a mixture of 'mud, wet lime, and sand, pressing it down firmly, and forming a squat hole and

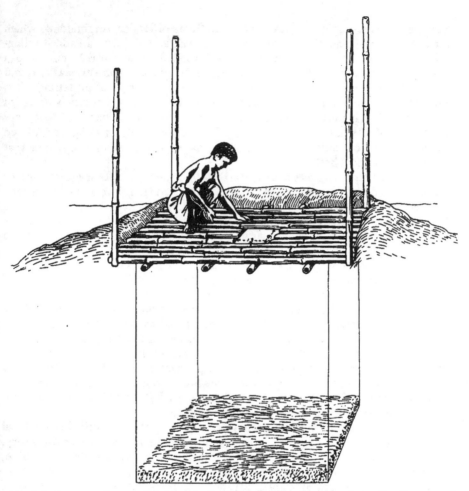

Fig.14. Constructing a pit latrine in Bangladesh. The diagram shows the framework of bamboo poles which will support the earthen floor. The squat hole measures 13 x 9 inches, that is 33 x 23 centimetres. The diagram also shows how a thick layer of grass, leaves, paper or straw is laid at the bottom of the latrine to encourage the formation of compost. (By courtesy of IVS Package Program, Ambarkhana, Sylhet.)

foot-rests'. The completed floor is finally plastered with thin, wet cement to make it waterproof.

A soil-cement floor slab of this kind is more satisfactory than an earthen floor without a hard surface, and may be recommended where people cannot afford concrete floor slabs. Even where no cement is used, however, some earth floors may be better than the experts assume, though they are often far from ideal. Techniques exist in parts of Africa for combining clay with other materials (e.g. cow-dung) to make plaster that will form a very hard and impermeable floor. In Zimbabwe and Botswana, techniques of this kind have been used in house building for five hundred years, and archaeologists have excavated the floors of very ancient buildings which are still hard and smooth. Similar techniques exist in Zaire, with an added refinement in places where there is little clay in the soil. The method is to mix cassava flour with soil and water in making the plaster for laying floors. This plaster is said to set like cement, and it is used regularly to make the floors of pit latrines. It is not entirely clear whether the resulting floor slabs are fully satisfactory with regard to hygiene, but it must be recognized that some indigenous materials have very remarkable properties which have never been scientifically investigated. All too often, experts from outside dismiss local techniques and materials, and assume that concrete or plastic is best.

Even accepting the virtues of some earthen floors, however, it may sometimes be relevant to consider covering them with plastic sheeting. This is a practice recommended by one agency in Bangladesh. An opened-out fertilizer sack provides a sheet of about the right size to cover a floor slab. A hole can be cut in the middle to expose the squat hole, and a mat laid on top of the plastic sheet is then used to hold it in place.

When deciding whether earthen floor slabs should be recommended for a particular area, the specific health problems of the locality must be taken into consideration. In stool samples taken in one part of Zaire (ZAI 32), some 48 per cent of all parasites identified were hookworm and 29 per cent were roundworm. These are the very infections most likely to be harboured by the earthen latrine floors used in that area, and experts warn that unsuitable latrines can positively increase their transmission. In 1979, when the author raised this point with medical staff responsible for the Zaire projects, they emphasized that hookworm larvae only develop in *moist* earth. The larvae die if the latrine floors are kept dry and every precaution is therefore taken to ensure that the earth floors in latrines remain dry, and that they are cleaned by sweeping, not by washing.

The use of earthen floors with this precaution is probably justified in the local circumstances of rural Zaire, but in most other places it will not be satisfactory. All too often, latrine floors are not kept sufficiently dry; splashing with urine, especially by children, is almost inevitable. In addition, roundworm eggs may survive for long periods even on a dry floor, and in some countries, the users of simple latrines are found to have a higher incidence of infection with this parasite than people who do not use latrines. Roundworms cannot get into people's bodies via their feet, but the eggs may be picked up on the hands of anyone (especially children) who touches the floor accidentally when they squat to defecate. For this reason, all latrines should ideally have a very smooth floor that is not porous so that the roundworm eggs will not be left behind when the latrine is cleaned. Most earth floors do not meet this requirement.

Design of privy huts

The design of the floor slab in any low-cost latrine is very much a technical problem, though it can also affect the social acceptability of the latrine. In complete contrast, though, the privy hut built on top of the floor slab presents few technical problems, but its design has a lot to do with whether people like the latrine and use it regularly, or whether they reject it. For example, the shape of the privy hut may be largely immaterial to the sanitation engineer, but may have much to do with whether the latrine is pleasant and attractive to use. The appearance of the hut may also seem irrelevant, but a neat, modern design may reflect people's aspirations for a better standard of living and their sense that prestige is involved in owning a latrine.

Some detailed points which affect the attractiveness of latrines to users have already been mentioned, including the question of whether a squat hole or a seat is provided. A smelly latrine is obviously unpleasant, but as already mentioned, a vent pipe can be installed (Fig.9). In addition, ample ventilation spaces should be left between the walls and the roof of the hut.

Other factors which determine whether people like the privy hut will include the amount of privacy it offers and its size. Very small privy huts sometimes induce claustrophobic feelings in users, and may be unhygienic if people are forced to touch the walls frequently. The size of the compartment and whether it has a door may be questions subject to strongly-held preferences, which can only be discovered by discussion with the people. Desirable fixtures inside the privy hut could include two handles for balance when squatting, a hook for clothes, or possibly a shelf for

Fig.15. Illustration used in health education work in Zaire showing a privy hut built of concrete blocks. Huts at rural pit latrines are more often built of local materials.

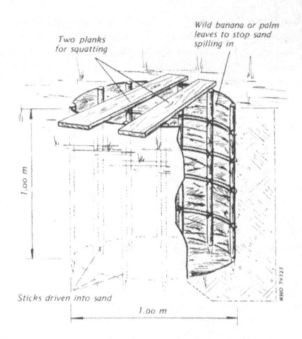

Fig. 16. Latrine without privy hut used in Mozambique — an attempt to deal with the needs of a very poor community. The latrine can be made by a woman in a day, and lasts 4-6 months. It is used like a trench latrine: earth is sprinkled on the fresh excreta to prevent access by flies. But the latrine is not easy for young children to use, and in many rural communities would not provide significant advantage over defecation in the open. (By courtesy of WHO: from Appropriate Technology for Health, Newsletter No.3, 1979.)

Two planks for squatting

Wild banana or palm leaves to stop sand spilling in

1.00 m

Sticks driven into sand

1.00 m

garments or the contents of pockets. However, all such fittings should be kept to a minimum, since they will all be touched with unwashed hands, and infection may be passed on unless they are frequently and thoroughly cleaned.

Brightness of the interior

The question of how light or dark the privy hut should be may also be important to local people. In one country, people positively expressed a preference for huts with windows. Dark huts are said to keep flies away, but may also discourage thorough cleaning. Thought should also be given to how the hut will be lit at night. Will users carry a light with them, and if so, whereabouts in the hut will it stand?

Choosing materials

In many places, privy huts are built from local materials by the owners of the latrines, who can therefore design the huts to suit their own individual tastes. Elsewhere, however, people will look on the latrine as part of the modernization of their home, and will want to build it with modern materials (Fig.15). In Botswana, for example, even where people are content with the very excellent local materials for their houses, they are willing to buy prefabricated privy huts made largely of corrugated iron (Fig.2). On the other hand, it is obviously a mistake to build a privy hut that is so smart that people will not dare defecate in it for fear of spoiling its pristine modernity. The latter mistake can best be avoided by not subsidizing the privy hut. This will encourage people to build what is within their means, which will then usually be compatible with their housing. The floor slab, however, may often be justifiably subsidized. If housing conditions are very poor, it may be

61

appropriate to provide a supply of corrugated iron paid for partly by a subsidy or a savings or loan scheme. In that case, people should be allowed to decide for themselves whether to use the corrugated iron on their houses or on privy huts. The point at issue, already raised in Chapter 2, is that latrines cannot sensibly be dealt with separately from housing. If people are too poor to afford reasonable houses, improvements in housing will be necessary if they are to achieve better hygiene. Latrines may not be appropriate until the people have better homes — or if latrines are appropriate, they may have to be very simple indeed (Fig.16). Only, however, in extreme conditions can these very basic types of latrine offer real benefits to a rural community.

Choice of site

The choice of a site for a latrine is another factor related to housing, and another point on which the wishes of the community may be crucial. Privies should not be too close to water sources; the minimum distance, usually quoted as 30 metres, must also depend on local rocks and soils. In limestone, for instance, disease carrying organisms may travel much further than in fine soils. Latrines might need to be within a certain minimum distance from houses if they are to be used at night. However, unless they are very well-ventilated and free from flies, they should be at least 6 metres from the house itself. Cultural factors may also influence not only the site of latrines, but also the way in which they face. In Moslem communities, privies should not face towards Mecca, and other groups may have preferences based on the desire for privacy.

5. Evaluation of Results

Monitoring long-term benefits

The danger of thinking in terms of 'projects' and 'programmes' (as in this booklet) is that these terms imply targets one hopes to reach in a limited time, and what happens afterwards is not discussed. But clearly, if one has, for example, encouraged people to wash their hands following defecation, this must become a permanent habit. If improvements in food hygiene have been encouraged, one must equally hope that these will become an established part of the housewife's routine. Logically, then, a project should never end completely; it should be followed up by an appraisal or evaluation of its long-term achievements. Then, if improvements in sanitation have not been sustained, or if new problems have emerged, there should be a continuing capability to assist people in surmounting these difficulties. In other words, projects are best undertaken as part of the activities of a health service which will be working in the community permanently, and which will be continually seeking to maintain existing standards of public health and improve them. There is little point, for example, in a two-year sanitation programme in a place where no further support can be provided after the project formally ends.

Following up projects

Where sanitation work has been supported by an established health service, the activities of its staff will provide an immediate means by which the outcome of the work can be checked. Health service staff keep records of the number of patients attending clinics and of the diseases they have. Thus, if changes in sanitation have made any impact on excreta-related illness, this should be noticeable in the routine statistics. It is not, however, a precise way of monitoring changes, because the number of patients attending clinics is liable to vary for all sorts of extraneous reasons. Ideally, a base-line survey of the prevalence of disease, involving house-to-house visits, will have been made before the start of the project. An exact survey can then be made later to see whether any change has occurred. The repeat survey should be made at the same time of year as the original study, because some diseases — especially diarrhoeal infections — vary in incidence with the seasons.

Significant improvements in a community's health should not be expected until a 'package' of related improvements in hygiene has been adopted. Latrines by themselves are not likely to cause much change unless their introduction is followed by more regular washing, better food hygiene, medical treatment for some of the worm infections, and other measures. But where latrines have been constructed, it is particularly important that they should be absorbed into the local culture, and become part of the people's lifestyle. If this does not happen, they may well be abandoned as soon as the sanitation experts depart, or when repairs are needed.

Social aspects

If new techniques are really to become part of a people's lifestyle, then we need to think of them as being *transformed* from something that is imported and alien into something that truly belongs to the local community. There are at least four main factors in the way projects are organized which have a part in determining whether this transformation actually takes place. Three of them have already been mentioned, but are worth repeating. First is the need to start with the resources that people already have, rather than with some idealistic notion of what they ought to have. That is why the need for careful appraisal of the local situation before work begins has been emphasized, looking particularly at local technology, such as techniques for making pottery, granaries, and earthen floors.

Second is the fundamental question of whether there is agreement about the purposes which the latrines are meant to serve — whether they will be built solely to benefit health, or whether they should also produce fertilizer or fit into a wider scheme of improved amenity.

Next comes discussion with local people about the detailed design of the latrines. This should cover the question of whether seats or squat-holes are preferred, whether the privy huts should be large or small, well-lit or dark, and where the latrines should be situated. Much of this discussion can take place on-site, especially where people intend to build the privy huts themselves.

What one now needs to consider is the fourth and final stage in transforming the latrines into something which belongs to the local people. This comes when the latrines are complete and are first being used. As people adopt new hygiene routines, due to the latrines, unforeseen problems may emerge. Fittings inside the privy hut may turn out to be badly placed; people may feel that their visits to the latrine are too publicly visible; traditional cleaning materials may prove inadequate; the water supply may be too far away, discouraging people from rinsing down the floor slab thoroughly. Sometimes the people will modify the latrine on their own initiative, perhaps moving fittings inside the hut, or adding a screen wall on the outside. Sometimes they may modify their hygiene routine unexpectedly, perhaps to avoid using the latrine after dark, or perhaps to fetch their water at different times. They may obtain a new water container, or new cleaning materials, or make other changes so that the latrine can be satisfactorily used.

Very often, these developments will take place without any outside stimulus as the people become more accustomed to the latrine and incorporate it into their way of life. But often, too, there will be difficulties that they cannot surmount by themselves, or there will be changes required for successful use of the latrine which they do not wish to make. It is in those circumstances that the latrines may be misused or entirely abandoned. One purpose of monitoring people's reaction to latrines after they are completed, and of continuing with health education, is to record and learn from any distinct improvement made, and to note any negative trends, so that action may be taken before the latrines are abandoned.

Evaluation of latrines

All too often, the experts who plan sanitation programmes are employed on short-term contracts, and disappear from the scene as soon as the latrines are complete. That is a mistake, because the dialogue which should take place between experts and local people needs to continue beyond construction. After the latrines are in use, there can still be dialogue, and of a very practical kind, because when the people modify their latrines, their actions are a comment on the success of the design which experts should find invaluable.

Where simple types of pit latrine have been built, one aim of the project should be to persuade people that this type of privy is something they can build themselves. Where more elaborate kinds of latrine have been installed, local builders should afterwards be able to contract for the construction of the latrines on their own account. Comments about latrines becoming part of the local culture are not just rhetoric; they refer to the need for the building and use of latrines to be perpetuated by individuals and institutions *within* the community. The reason why the public health service should keep an eye on the use and maintenance of latrines after their completion is partly to assess whether this aim has been met.

Points which should be particularly noted at this stage can be summarized as follows:

a. Are the latrines used regularly, at night as well as by day?
b. Do all the members of each family use them?
c. Are they regularly and thoroughly cleaned?
d. If different types of latrine have been built, which are most regularly used, which are kept cleanest, and which do the people say they prefer?
e. What modifications have been made to the latrines?
f. What materials, brushes, etc., do people use for cleaning latrines?
g. Is refuse put into latrines?
h. How quickly are latrine pits (or composting compartments) filling up?
i. Are any structural faults emerging?
j. When a new house is built, do people build a latrine to go with it, as a matter of course?

If these questions are asked during a continuing health education programme, suggestions and improvements made by particularly enterprising latrine owners can be passed on to other people. Health workers should emphasize the cleaning of latrines, and where their efforts to monitor this reveal difficulties, there may again be need for technical assistance. For example, if suitable brushes or mops are lacking, efforts could be made to ensure that such articles are made in the community, or are otherwise available for purchase. But the use of strong disinfectants should not usually be encouraged, because they interfere with the natural decomposition of excreta in nearly all types of latrine.

One critical point to watch will be how quickly latrine pits fill up, and how often aqua-privies need desludging. With aqua-privies and composting latrines, long-term success depends on desludging or the clearance of compost being carried out regularly. Some kind of back-up service is needed for aqua-privy desludging. This is often provided by local government authorities who have proper equipment for the job, but unless project staff liaise with such bodies, the work is likely to be neglected. It should be noted, however, that a novel aqua-privy has recently been introduced with a view to simplifying the desludging operation. This is built with its tank entirely above ground level and with steps leading up to the privy hut. A valve is provided at the bottom of the tank for desludging by gravity flow.

By contrast, pit latrines are cheap to build, and when one becomes full, it is simply replaced by a new one. When dug in sandy soils replacement may be necessary every two years; but deep pits in firm soil have been known to last ten or fifteen years. Two practices which may shorten a pit's life, though, are the use of solid materials for anal cleaning and the disposal of rubbish in the pit.

Conclusion

The whole purpose of any sanitation project, whether it leads to the building of latrines or not, is to secure permanent improvements in cleanliness, in the disposal of wastes, and in hygiene habits. There is no point in persuading people to go through a routine simply to please an outside expert if they forget it as soon as he goes away. What is wanted is a change that people will take into their own culture and accept as part of their lifestyle, and which will benefit their health for always.

An outside agency may hope to *stimulate* a change of this kind, but very obviously only the people can carry it through. It is essential, therefore, to start with the assets that the people already have, and with their own aspirations. It is essential to work out improvements in hygiene and sanitation which build on the more positive customs and beliefs they have, which use the material resources they own, and which help them achieve some of their own social goals. An outsider can only contribute to this process by being willing to learn from the local community as well as to advise; and by noting and encouraging their innovative abilities, perhaps helping them through some kind of technical assistance programme.

Bibliography

Books Available From: Intermediate Technology Publications Ltd., 9 King Street, London, WC2E 8HN, England.

S. Cairncross and R. Feachem, *Small Water Supplies*, 1978, (a Ross Institute handbook on village water supply).

Katherine Elliott, *The Training of Auxiliaries in Health Care*, 1975, (a comprehensive list of resources available in 1975 for training village health workers and other auxiliaries).

R. Feachem, M. McGarry and D. Mara, *Water, Wastes and Health in Hot Climates*, 1977, (a wide-ranging book for planners published by John Wiley but available from Intermediate Technology Publications).

R. Feachem and S. Cairncross, *Small Excreta Disposal Systems*, 1978, (a very useful booklet from the Ross Institute covering most low-cost latrines).

O. Gish *et al.*, *Health Manpower and the Medical Auxiliary*, 1971, (a short book with useful material on health education and village health workers).

H.T. Mann and D. Williamson, *Water Treatment and Sanitation*, 1976, (a short book on sanitation technology relevant to the larger rural communities).

Krisno Nimpuno, *The Vietnamese Toilet*, 1980, (to be published in *Appropriate Technology*, the journal of the Intermediate Technology Development Group).

Arnold Pacey, *Gardening for Better Nutrition*, 1978, (includes material on health education and technical assistance).

TOOL Foundation, *The Preparation of Soap*, 1976 (six-page leaflet).

VITA, *Village Technology Handbook*, 1975, (a very practical American publication with sections on latrines, water supply, and food technology).

S.B. Watt and W.E. Wood, *Hand Dug Wells and their Construction*, 1977, (the best available handbook on wells).

S.B. Watt, *Ferrocement Water Tanks and their Construction*, 1978, (a handbook describing the water tanks mentioned in Chapters 2 and 3).

Other Books Mentioned

H.H.D. Attfield, *Composting Privy*, 1977, (Bulletin No.1 from IVS Package Program, Ambarkhana, Sylhet, Bangladesh).

Donald Curtis, 'Values of latrine users and administrators', in *Sanitation in Developing Countries*, edited by A. Pacey, 1978.

R. Feachem, D. Bradley, H. Garelick and D. Mara, *Sanitation and Disease; Health Aspects of Excreta and Wastewater Management*, 1980, (an authoritative and comprehensive book produced for the World Bank and due shortly from Johns Hopkins University Press, Baltimore).

H. Guggenheim and R. Fanale, 'Shared technology: a project for water storage and irrigation in Dogon villages', *African Environment Occasional Paper*, No.76-1, March 1976.

P. Hawkins and R. Feachem, 'An engineering view of certain helminth (worm) infections', in *Sanitation in Developing Countries*, edited by A. Pacey, 1978.

Joan K. McMichael, *Health in the Third World: Studies from Vietnam*, 1976, (Spokesman Books, Nottingham).

Arnold Pacey (editor), *Sanitation in Developing Countries*, 1978, (John Wiley & Sons, Chichester and New York).

W. Rybczynski, C. Polprasert, and M.McGarry, *Low-cost Technology Options for Sanitation*, International Development Research Centre, Ottawa, 1978.

E.G. Wagner and J.P. Lanoix, *Excreta Disposal for Rural Areas and Small Communities*, 1958, (World Health Organization, Geneva).

Printed in the USA
CPSIA information can be obtained
at www.ICGtesting.com
JSHW012045140824
68134JS00034B/3276